Adventure Skiing

Dave Wynne-Jones

ENDORSEMENTS

"*Adventure Skiing* is a great title for a book that encapsulates all that is great in the sport of skiing, from carving on a piste to making the first turns off piste then discovering the magic of ski touring that can take you anywhere in the world with mountains and snow. Dave Wynne-Jones shares his progression from climber and alpinist to skier, ski mountaineer and adventure skier. The format of the book is a great model for the reader to discover their own love of the sport; days tours lead to a desire for more adventure; hut to hut tours in Europe lead further afield to crossings of unexplored mountain ranges and the ascent of unclimbed peaks.

Dave's anecdotal style allows the reader to enjoy the adventure but also learn from Dave's experiences, *Adventure Skiing* is a book to be enjoyed and an inspiration for planning our own adventures in the snowy mountains."

– BRUCE GOODLAD, MOUNTAIN GUIDE
AND AUTHOR OF SKI-TOURING.

"In his new book Dave draws on his wealth of experience to describe the variety of options open to the ski-tourer, from resort-based day tours to fully self-sufficient expeditions. Each account illustrates not just the pleasures and the pitfalls, the joys and the hazards encountered but also the part played by group dynamics and interpersonal relations within a team. Every skier will find something of interest here."

– ROB COLLISTER, MOUNTAIN GUIDE
AND AUTHOR OF DAYS TO REMEMBER.

"Dave draws on decades of experience as a skier and mountaineer to show how skis can be used to facilitate travel, exploration and climbing around the world detailing the different challenges, risks and rewards of ski expeditions."

– DAVID HAMILTON, MOUNTAIN GUIDE.

Whittles Publishing Ltd
An imprint of Porto Press Ltd,
3 Connaught Road
St Albans
AL3 5RX

www.portopress.co.uk

© 2026 Dave Wynne-Jones

ISBN: 9781849956147

Cover and text design by Raspberry Creative Type, Edinburgh

Printed by 4Edge

Also by
Dave Wynne-Jones

The Way Taken – A Chinese Expedition
Delfryn Publications: ISBN 978-9163674-1-8

4000m: Climbing the Highest Mountains of the Alps
Whittles Publishing 2016: ISBN 978-184995-172-2

An Expedition Handbook with Mountaineering Case Studies
Whittles Publishing 2023: ISBN 978-184995-535-5

CONTENTS

PARTICIPATION STATEMENT

The author and the publisher recognise that Adventure Skiing is a sport with a risk of injury or death. Participants in Adventure Skiing should be aware of and accept these risks, and take responsibility for their own actions.

This book is dedicated to all those who have joined me in these and other adventures on ski (you know who you are!) and also to the memory of Denis Mitchell and Jeremy Whitehead who in their different ways shared some great days out with me.

ACKNOWLEDGEMENTS

I should like to thank a number of people for their support in the writing of this book.

The various editors of journals and magazines in which accounts of some of these adventures were published over the years, including Steve Goodwin (Alpine Journal), John Harlin III, Kelly Cordes and Lindsay Griffin (American Alpine Journal), David Seddon, Mike and Jenny Spencer, Mike Hendry (Eagle Ski Club Yearbook), Geoff Birtles and Ian Smith (High magazine).

Derek Buckle former vice-president of the Alpine Club who read the first draft of the book, whilst he and Howard Pollitt contributed to the maps provided for the Ak-Shirak Expeditions.

The Mount Everest Foundation, Alpine Club and Eagle Ski Club for supporting the Ak-Shirak expeditions with grants.

Keith Whittles for his faith in the book and Diane Page at Porto Press for keeping that faith. My editor, Caroline Petherick, for her enthusiasm, rigor and willingness to discuss the editorial issues when working together on this book.

All those fellow-adventurers who have kept me company on this journey.

PREFACE

Skiing is fun. Learning about balance, controlling direction and speed, making turns; the learning itself is fun, although sometimes the laughter of a spill can evaporate in the pain of its consequences, which may turn out to be serious. Skiing requires both fitness and co-ordination of mind and body in an attempt to manage what is essentially a controlled fall, sliding down a mountain. Control is the key to unlock enjoyment, but we should never forget that the attraction of the mountain setting plays a major part in the satisfaction of the sport. Without mountains there would be no snowy slopes to ski, though there might be skiing in lands where deep winter snows would otherwise prevent people getting about. Rolling terrain of that nature has been skied by hunters from prehistoric times; it's more like the Nordic skiing that can be seen in the Winter Olympics, particularly the races that incorporate target shooting at checkpoints along the track.

When the basic skills have been acquired, skiers challenge themselves with faster, steeper descents, moguls, glacier skiing, near-piste and off-piste runs in perfect powder (or not!) and the development of more advanced skills leading to a fluent style that can better cope with the demands of the terrain. Every skier knows when they are skiing well, achieving 'flow'. The body's feedback through the rhythm of the descent tells them, and it's an experience that transcends the limitations of everyday life. 'There is something almost sexual about powder skiing,' Dougal Haston reckoned, and he should know. Orgasmic skiing? Serious fun!

Challenge is an intrinsic part of that fun, but as the scale of the challenge increases, so does the element of risk. Sliding down a mountain is fun when it's controlled, painful when it's not, and some skiers draw a line beyond which they are not prepared to take on the risks involved.

For some it may be black runs, for others off-piste; when skiing in and around ski resorts there is usually sufficient information available to make good judgements about the level of risk. Signs indicate where the difficult runs are, and even off-piste there is information available about the snowpack so that avalanche risk can be managed. Off-piste runs have usually been skied by others, so there may well be tracks, and information from those others posted online or exchanged over a drink in a bar. But that's not adventure skiing.

Adventure skiing is when skiing in and around a ski resort is no longer enough, when skiers seek situations in which there is less information, more uncertainty about the outcome, more demands on their skills and judgement; plans may need to be adapted and theories tested, and with that uncertainty the risk level is higher. In adventure skiing the mountain looms larger. No longer tamed by technology, patrolled by security experts, colonised by fast food outlets, the mountain confronts the skier on a one-to-one basis and in doing so forges a closer, richer relationship.

In practice the relationship is rarely one to one. The risk would be higher than the majority of skiers would accept. Most adventure skiing is a team activity, and that too enhances the relationships of those skiers with each other, playing to the strengths of the team and compensating for individual weaknesses, as well as benefiting from other perspectives on their developing relationship with the mountains.

Moving outside the charmed circle of the ski resort means giving up an enormous privilege; that of gaining, without the slightest effort, the height necessary to ski down time after time. I'm not knocking it! Lift-assisted skiing has given me lots of fun over the years, and I still tend to have a warm-up day in resort in order to let the team get their 'ski legs' back before going off to have adventures. To gain the skill level to be able to ski off-piste takes years of practice, and that practice would take many more years if it meant walking uphill every time a skier wanted to learn from a descent.

At a time when the Climate Crisis is posing an existential threat to our species, even in the best-case scenario there's going to be a lot less snow around. That's why ski stations are fitting racks for mountain bikes to their chairlifts and installing snowmaking equipment for their lower runs. The earlier boom in ski station building, with more apartment blocks and larger lifts capable of conveying many more people to the departure points for ski runs, caters for more people – but the actual number of runs hasn't increased much, if at all. That's created over-crowding on piste, particularly in the high season when that increasingly expensive lift pass just leads to more time spent in lift queues and skiing crowded pistes; that's not good value for money, nor much fun at times. Ski stations are in danger of pricing themselves out of the market.

The result has been an increased interest in ski-touring, which has been reflected in the decisions of mountain provinces like Aragon in Spain to staff more huts all the year round to cater for skiers visiting those huts in the less extreme weather of modern winters. When Covid-19 shut down the ski resorts, it was remarkable how many skiers turned to ski-mountaineering equipment to get themselves up and down the slopes, and how few complained about the lack of groomed pistes. Lack of snow simply encouraged those adventurers to go and look for it in the many mountains and valleys unsuitable for ski resorts.

When skiing was first developed there was no alternative to walking uphill, carrying skis or using sealskins attached to the underside of the skis, which created sufficient adhesion to climb on ski, by zigzagging when the steepness of the slope demanded it. Then roads and railways arrived, and it was possible to take a bus or train to a higher village and ski back to your base. As the popularity of the sport increased, the technology developed and ski-lifts revolutionised skiing, in the process taking much of the adventure out of it. To regain that adventure is to move back into a relationship with the mountains, which means getting up them by your own efforts.

Adventure skiing is a form of mountaineering.

It's still fun!

An unexpected adventure on-piste

A note on the technicalities

Increasing the risk level on-piste

The key to 'uphill skiing' is the **skin.** Modern technology has developed strips of material cut to the footprint of the ski, with a sticky side that holds the skin to the ski and the other side textured with a nap like moleskin, which stroked one way resists movement but stroked the other way slides easily. Slid forward, the ski moves across the surface of the snow, but when it is weighted as the other ski is slid forward, the skin's nap grips and does not slide backwards. Modern glue sticks the skin to the base of the ski yet enables the skier to forcibly strip the skin from the ski for descent and reuse later for further ascents. Ski-mountaineering bindings also assist by releasing the heel to enable a normal walking action in ascent whilst locking the heel down for descent. Dedicated boots will also have a walking and skiing setting for uphill and downhill use.

A PERSONAL PROGRESSION

My first attempt at skiing ended in the worst haematoma that the nurse attached to our group had ever seen; a black carbuncle rising from deep purples of bruising around the right hip. Whether it had been my ski instructor's accent or mine, communication with him was almost non-existent whilst I was accompanying my school party. I learnt little, but was so anxious not to hold up the group that I crashed far too often for my health.

After that there were no plans to repeat the experience until a good friend, Ceri Jones, talked me into joining a team going to Kitzbühel. There I had to learn to ski by trial and error, because by the time I'd paid for the holiday, ski pass and ski hire there was no money left for lessons.

It helped to observe other skiers closely and to talk about what had been going wrong for me with independent skiers in the group back at the chalet every evening. Al, another friend, generously offered to smuggle me into his instructor's group for a sample lesson. I was tempted and gave it a try, but after patiently waiting at a succession of ski-tows for one or other member of the group to stop falling over, I decided that I spent a great deal more time actually skiing when skiing on my own. The ski pass wasn't cheap, and value for money was a priority.

Al planned to settle the fees issue by not attending his next group lesson, so I suggested we team up next day. We skied a lot, and at the end of that day Al decided he too was learning more by skiing more; he never went back to his lessons. We could watch and comment on what each other was doing wrong, benefiting from another perspective, as well as pushing each other with a little healthy competition. It was also fun. To the surprise of the rest of the group, we were both skiing parallel, more or less, by the end of the week.

For the next ten years I skied with friends and family every year, but never had another lesson. Once my wife had gone back to work and the kids were old enough to join us, my winter climbing gave way to family ski holidays, taking on off-piste challenges as well as fulfilling the objective of 'skiing black runs, fast, with style'. During those ten years I also served my apprenticeship in summer alpinism, which supplied all the snow and ice that I wished to climb.

Then in 1990 another friend, Paddy Feeley, put a team together to visit Chamonix and 'try out this ski-touring malarkey'. With scant experience, again we learnt by trial and error, and I remember Mike Cooper skiing elegantly past, off-piste at Le Tour, to head-plant spectacularly on the next turn. Descending from the Vignettes Hut after being pinned down for several days by storm, we had some discussion about whether or not we needed to take the skins off when descending in new snow conditions. Frustrated by the lack of progress, I removed mine and in more ways than one never looked back.

At Easter the following year, Denis Mitchell, Ralph Atkinson and I completed the Classic Haute Route from Chamonix to Zermatt via the Valsorey Hut and the Plateau de Couloir in just six days. It was our first hut-to-hut tour. It helped that we had all served our apprenticeships in alpine climbing. From then on, Easter was the time for exploring the high Alps on ski.

Clearly the search for adventure was rooted in the challenges posed by backcountry skiing, but with increasing experience and technical expertise such challenges can become less demanding; more of a nice day out appreciating the mountain scenery than an adventure. An adventure might still surprise us (the mountain environment is never completely predictable) but the quest for adventure remained, and I realised that it involved a progression. My appetite for adventure increased as experience and skills increased, and could be fed by the progression from day tours through hut-to-hut, multi-day traverses, to increasingly demanding expeditions.

Days out from valley bases can still provide an adventure, but opportunities are more likely to occur on extended hut-to-hut tours and are practically guaranteed in the remote and challenging destinations chosen for expeditions that might involve weeks of snow-camping traversing an entire mountain range for the first time. These have been some of the most fulfilling experiences of my life. I hope that the experiences related will encourage you to find adventure in your life, but always with the awareness that for all of us there are unacceptable risks – and there's no shame in recognising that.

DAY TOURS TO REMEMBER

1

THE BLACK MOUNT TRAVERSE – SCOTLAND

Some adventures can be sprung on you.

The telephone rang. It was Denis: 'Do you have anything planned for the May Bank Holiday this weekend?'

'Not really. I've had a few ideas, but the weather's been a bit changeable, so nothing definite.'

'Right, then. Do you fancy some skiing?'

'Oh, aye, great idea – but it's a bit far to the Alps for a long weekend,' I said, winding up my sarcasm.

'In Scotland?'

I lapsed into stunned silence, then: 'You *are joking*? Scotland? The land of torrential rain? And this is May we're talking about.'

'No, seriously. I've been following the weather patterns. There should still be plenty of snow high up in the west of Scotland, and there's frost forecast for this weekend.'

Now I had to take this seriously. Denis was an inveterate weather-watcher. He studied the subject over weeks, piecing together an ongoing picture of developing conditions for winter climbing or making canny suggestions for rock-climbing in the Lakes, Wales or the Peak District, based on the movement of weather fronts across the country. Taking notice of his recommendations had meant that we'd often salvaged some excellent days on the hills from weekend forecasts of foul weather.

His opinion was to be respected. But this was still Scotland we were contemplating.

'You still there?'

'Course. Have you phoned the ski centre in Glencoe?'

'Yeah. There's snow, and they're open all weekend.'

'Okay, what's the plan?'

'Well, we can get back our ski legs with a few hours on the tows at the White Corries, then ski the Black Mount Traverse. It's light till late at this time of year, and we can stay at the FRCC hut, Waters Cottage.'

I hesitated for a moment; the proposal still seemed a little crazy – but, hey, so was most of my life at the time. 'Okay, I'm in!'

So it was that Denis and I pulled into the White Corries car park and were hoisted above muddy moorland on the first chairlift, then trudged across more mud and slush to a further chair and tows. There was a chill in the air.

Suddenly we were stepping into our skis and sliding off on good snow. A couple of short runs from the chair loosened up our leg muscles, and we turned our attention to the higher tows. Only one was open, with the cable towing us along horizontally at about hip height, instead of running metres above our heads, because of the depth of snow. We could have jumped over the cable, and the top of the pylons was no more than 2 metres above the surface. The other tow was closed because there was so much snow that the crossbars of the pylons, from which the cables should have been suspended, barely cleared the surface. That meant there was a depth of an incredible 4–5 metres of snow. It wasn't evenly distributed, though.

At the top of the tow, we had to carry skis along rocky tracks windswept clear of snow to access runs in the 'Flypaper' area, but there was no problem about skiing every available run, several times. The weather held, and by mid-afternoon Denis and I were gazing from Meall a'Bhuiridh at white ridges stretching towards Clath Leathad and Stob Ghabhar.

'Time to give that traverse a try?' Denis queried.

'Why not?'

We slid off westwards, where walkers' tracks descended narrow snow tongues to a bealach, then rose to Point 1068m on the ridge from Sron na Creise to Clath Leathad. At the lowest point Denis shouldered his skis and set off, climbing between rocky outcrops by following footsteps kicked in the snow, with me close behind him. Gaining the crest of the ridge and fixing skins to the skis, we could skin easily south towards Clath Leathad. The cliffs of Coire an Easain to the east were capped with huge cornices, which in one place seemed to be on the point of collapse. A crevasse-like cornice break-line was given a wide berth as sunshine touched the snow with brightness. Far below, the tawny expanse of Rannoch Moor, mottled with cloud shadows, reminded me of the contrasting conditions found in the Scottish landscape in May.

Snow lay deepest along the eastern edge of the ridge, away from the rocks and scree laid bare by prevailing westerly winds. This was underscored by the descent from Clath Leathad, west towards Bealach Fuar-chathaidh, carrying skis again and booting through thin snow, following traces of a rocky path beneath.

Then we came upon the head of a steep gully dropping direct to a point a little east of the bealach. Within minutes we were back on ski, carving tight turns down perfect spring snow, finishing with an adrenalin high, so that we scarcely cared about having to remove skis again to traverse past a rocky knoll at the lowest point. Carrying skis, climbing the virtually snow-free ridge beyond, up to its junction with the main ridge of Aonach Mor, I looked back to see a rainbow arcing

Approaching Stob Ghabhar

out of the most unlikely of stormy skies with its base placed firmly at the foot of that gully – it was no pot of gold, but certainly a gift as far as we were concerned!

Back on ski, we found that the undulations of Aonach Mor offered no obstacles to continuous skinning for a couple of kilometres before climbing the north-west flank of Stob Ghabhar in bright sunshine under clearing skies. East of the summit, the evening's drop in temperature was crisping the snow as we cautiously lost height on the ridge bounding Coirein Lochain.

The classic Black Mount Traverse involves a descent south-east from Stob Ghabhar to Victoria Bridge, with a vehicle waiting there to return skiers to the White Corries car park. In current conditions, that descent was likely to involve a lot of walking and with only one car – back at the ski centre – Denis and I had been unable to make such transport arrangements. This was the one point about which Denis had been a bit vague in describing the plan.

Now he reckoned we needed to descend into Coirein Lochain, and that was why we were hesitating above the cornices. Trying to find a way through to the slopes beneath without triggering an avalanche that could sweep one or both of us away was no easy task. Despite the scepticism of continental skiers, avalanches are a very real hazard in Scotland.

After much toing and froing, peering at the cornices from different angles, we decided on the safest line, and I plunged over in a flurry of displaced snow to drop onto a steep traverse underneath the cornices. On closer inspection these proved less threatening than we had feared. Their shelves were buttressed by a build-up of snow beneath them. Nothing was triggered. When I reached a position clear of any cornice collapse, Denis followed,

Descending Coirein Lochain

exactly on the line. We then watched each other ski the pitches of the corrie headwall one at a time, noticing how much of each other's ski bases could be seen from below as we edged on steep névé.

As the slope eased above the lochan, which was hidden beneath deep snow, we followed the snowy course of the Allt Coire Dhearbhadh stream, flowing out of the lochain under the frozen surface. Fortunately snow conditions remained good enough for some technical weaving between boulders emerging from the snow and exposed tumps of grass and heather, but in places the purity of the surrounding whiteness was sullied by dirty slides of melted earthy debris. Near where the stream burst out from under the snow, we ran out of the snow patches that we had been linking to continue skiing. There was nothing for it but to lash skis onto our packs and walk out.

It was at this point that my faith in Denis's planning suffered a blow, as he casually revealed that there were 5 miles of bog, moorland and old military road back to the car park. To be walked in ski boots. I made a mental note to check the details better next time. Clouds were colouring up, pink and bronze, as the sun set out of sight behind a ridge, while we bog-hopped across an area ominously named The Moss, following the general course of the River Ba. Eventually we met the military road, now designated the West Highland Way, where Ba Bridge crossed the river.

The first of the military roads had been built by General Wade in the 1720s and 1730s to enable the English army to control the Highlands after the defeat of the Jacobite rebellion in 1715, but resistance had continued until the Battle of Culloden in 1745. Despite other officers being responsible for building later military roads, the network had become known as Wade's Roads. The West Highland Way has since become a way of bringing people together rather than a means of repression. Now the stony track rolled unpredictably through rough moorland as light faded from the sky. It was after 11 pm, in full darkness under a few twinkling stars, when we reached the car, alone in a deserted car park.

Eating late meant sleeping late next morning, so there was nothing for it but to wimp out and go cornice jumping into the eastern corries of Aonach Mor, unashamedly making use of the lift system. There were more crevasse-like cornice break-lines, but we ignored them and followed the tracks of previous skiers over safe, established jumps.

By Monday it was raining for the long drive home.

2

A QUEYRAS FIRST
DESCENT – FRANCE

Other adventures can suddenly shift into a higher gear of commitment.

En route to the Queyras in February 2009, Alex Hood and I stopped off to visit Françoise Call in Chamonix. Knut Tønsberg was also visiting, so the four of us had an acclimatisation day in the Vallée Blanche, taking the steep and exciting Envers du Plan variation. Above the Requin Hut we met a French guide and his clients who were so shaken by his fall into a crevasse that they asked Françoise if they could ski down with our party. Lacking both equipment and the knowledge of how to use it, the clients hadn't been able to rescue the guide, so he'd been very lucky to make radio contact with a mountain rescue team back at the Midi station, which had come and hauled him out of the crevasse. Seeing our party with crevasse-rescue gear on our harnesses, the guide had decided to increase the odds in his favour during the rest of his descent. Nothing untoward occurred, but it was a challenging warm-up run. Back at the chalet, Alex and I loaded up the Landrover to continue our journey that evening, arriving in Guillestre at 10 pm.

Phil Ingle was expecting Alex and me for an Alpine Club meet he had organised; John Kentish and Peter Moody had planned to fly out to join us later. Phil had moved from Chamonix to run the pension with his partner whilst also working on IT contracts. He was an enthusiast for steep skiing, who had skied in Chamonix with fellow

Descending the Envers du Plan variation of the Vallée Blanche

enthusiast Tomas Olsson, who I'd met on Pik Lenin (in Kyrgyzstan). Tomas had invited me to join his team on Muztagh Ata (in north-western China) in 2003, and Phil had also been invited onto that expedition but had had to drop out owing to other commitments.

Moving from Chamonix to the Queyras, he had been worried about whether there would be enough skiing to satisfy him in Guillestre. It had turned out to be far quieter than Chamonix, so that there was none of the frantic racing for fresh tracks he'd encountered there. Good powder was often still left untracked to be skied days after snowfall.

Unfortunately, Phil found himself having to deal with an unexpected additional amount of work, so pointed Alex and me in the direction of some recommended tours while he was unable to get out with us.

A late start at Ceillac saw us taking the chairlift and tow, then aiming to skin on up to the Col du Petit Part. Unfortunately, our aim was off and we found ourselves at the Col du Girardin, so traversed south along the ridge and skied around a bowl to reach the base of the broad couloir falling from the Col du Petit Part. Skinning up to the first col in the sunshine was delightful, but the bowl was in shadow and we needed to use harscheisen to climb to the second.

But Alex on ascending was having trouble that was not easy to pin down; perhaps it was the weight of his skis or the narrowness of his skins, which didn't fully cover the ski base. He never quite made it to the top, and when the sun dipped behind a ridge I became too cold to wait any longer for him so skied down while he took off skins and harscheisen before he also skied down to join me.

Low temperatures meant crusting snow on a traverse above the lake and past a little chapel that took us back to the piste, and thence to the car by 6 pm. It had been a good choice as a warm-up tour, usefully revealing some gear problems for Alex, but never quite warm enough for me in the cold shadows.

Next day we skinned up from La Rua to the Col des Prés du Fromage, then north to Sommet Bucher, 2254m, which seemed to be popular with snow-shoers coming up through the woods; a pair of game old girls were taking a break at the Clôt Henri, a tidy little bivouac hut with a good iron stove, when we took a look inside. There should have been powder skiing through the trees but the frozen crust was more character-building than enjoyable, so there was only one descent. Later, Phil expressed surprise that the powder hadn't lasted longer.

The following day Alex and I returned to Ceillac with designs on the Tête du Rissace, but we didn't get far before discovering that Alex had a broken binding, not repairable in the field. Continuing up the track for a little way, we found a sunny spot for lunch before skiing carefully back to the car in order to sort out the binding at the ski shop in Guillestre. The cost of a replacement part plus a week's ski hire, while the part was in transit, would cost more than a new pair of bindings, which could be fitted immediately. Alex bought new bindings.

It was lucky that we hadn't been halfway through a hut-to-hut tour when these gear problems had surfaced, but so far so good. Alex and I were playing ourselves in steadily to our first ski-touring of the season, sorting out kit issues on undemanding tours – very manageable, very low-key – while waiting for the full team to arrive.

Back at the pension, Phil had got on better than expected with his work, and proposed joining us next day. He was not surprised about the binding problem, and had steered clear of that particular brand after a toepiece fell into two halves just after he had skied an exposed gnarly pitch in Chamonix. If it had broken whilst he was skiing, he reckoned he'd have been killed.

'I use Alpine Trekker binding adapters,' Phil explained, 'that fit into downhill bindings and give me heel lift on the ascent, but I can stow them in my rucksack and rely on the downhill bindings for the descent.'

'What about the boots?' Alex asked. 'Don't you need downhill boots for downhill bindings, which won't be very safe on mixed ground or booting up steep snow?'

'Yes, I do use downhill boots for the precision and support, but a local cobbler fits Vibram soles to them. Not the most comfortable in ascent but I've seen feet damaged by ill-fitting ski-mountaineering boots much worse than I've ever suffered.'

That was a very high-spec and idiosyncratic set-up, I thought to myself.

As we talked into the evening, Phil made us an offer: 'You know, living round here I get the chance to scope out routes that aren't the usual thing, and I've been looking at this particular couloir for a while. I think it's in condition now, so how do you fancy making a first ski descent?'

'How hard?' was my immediate response. It had been three years since I'd skied a technical couloir.

'Not very. I think. Hard to tell until we climb it. But if you don't fancy it, when we get to the top there's a col just below the summit with two options to ski back to Le Coin; south via the Ravin de Clapouse, or north via the Lac du Lauzon, both established ski routes.'

Climbing Pic du Jaillon

'I'd be up for it.' Alex was keen.

'I'm not sure after seeing how different your ski set-up is, Phil,' I was doubtful. 'I've only lightweight skis and bindings. Are they going to be up to the demands of the skiing?'

We went to check out my kit before Phil decided, 'I think you'll manage on those.'

'Okay, I'll take a look. Yes, why not?' I was persuaded, though I was well aware that this was a major step up in the seriousness of the trip.

An early start found us skinning up from Le Coin, just north of Arvieux, at 9.15 am, climbing pleasantly through a narrow, wooded valley to emerge onto more open slopes above. At about 2000m we trended left below cliffs to keep to snow slopes thinning into white seams in the rocky east face of the Pic du Jaillon. Above the cliffs one of those seams was the line of the couloir that Phil intended to ski, falling from just right of the summit, but finishing at the top of the cliffs we were skirting. We would need to find a way of traversing into it above the cliffs.

As the slope steepened, skins, harscheisen and anything else deemed to be excess were stashed, and skis strapped to our rucksacks. Then we began booting up in the direction of a broader break in the cliffs on the left. The break ended in a shallow bowl with a steep, awkward exit over rocks to a rib. Gaining our couloir appeared to be decidedly precarious at that point. Climbing with skis was a difficult enough balancing act at the best of times, so we soloed on up a parallel couloir with Phil in the lead hoping to find an easier traverse higher up.

Narrow snow gullies and rocky ribs continued to offer a line of ascent, but still no way of slipping into the couloir we'd intended to climb. The climbing was steep enough to yield some spectacular pictures, and eventually we found ourselves breaking through a cornice onto the summit ridge about 30m right of the highest point. From there it was clear that the entry to our couloir lay below and to the right. We had entirely avoided the line of our couloir in the ascent! That was actually something of a relief to me, because I had no confidence that I'd have been able to ski the line that we had climbed.

Barring our way to the couloir entry was a steep and loose-looking rock step. Phil stared down at it for a minute or so, then announced,

Climbing the summit ridge of Pic du Jaillon

'There's no way that we're climbing down there with skis on our backs.' Neither Alex nor I disagreed.

We sat in the snow, enjoying the sunshine, eating lunch and discussing options, though the only real one was to head for the summit. Fortunately, the ridge to the summit was straightforward enough, although we had to continue a little way beyond the summit cross to reach a point where we could step into our bindings to descend steeply to the Col de Combe Laboye. There more discussion of options took place.

'So, which of the escape routes are we going to take?' I asked, 'South via the Ravin du Clapouse, or north, skirting the Crête du Jaillon and passing the Cabane de la Gardère?'

Phil was not so easily deflected from our objective, 'Well there is a third alternative; to ski north, keeping as high as possible in order to climb up to the couloir entry point. The step in the ridge should be a good indicator of where to aim for.'

'But we left our skins below the cliffs,' Alex protested.

'Yes; we'll just have to lose as little height as possible on the traverse, then it'll be a bootpack up to the ridge. Hopefully a short one.'

It made sense, and I could see that Phil was convinced that the couloir was skiable. 'Okay. Let's give it a go.'

Once established at the head of the couloir, we had time to prepare ourselves for the descent. Psychologically we were at a disadvantage; instead of skiing what we had climbed we were going to be entering unknown territory. Dropping into an initial snow slope of at least 50 degrees, beginning with a bulge that was probably windslab, was daunting, but thankfully there was no cornice. I was intimidated enough on my lightweight touring gear to have absolutely no desire for first tracks! Both Alex and Phil were better equipped, with heavier duty skis and bindings, particularly Phil with his specialised set-up for exactly this sort of skiing.

'Only one rule,' said Phil, 'never put in a turn above someone below you.' Then he was off, to smash out a line through the windslab. Alex followed, and when a shout came up from below, I knew it was my turn.

Initially side-slipping, I put in turn after turn where the couloir opened out and the angle eased a little. It had been three years since I'd been on anything as steep as this, so I had to consciously override the tendency to flinch from the steepness.

Joining the others in a safe niche that Phil had identified, out of the line of any potential avalanche, it was clear that we were committed. One at a time, we skied pitch after pitch, on mostly good snow, with Phil spotting other islands of safety, and Alex and I slotting in below the skier ahead where they had found shelter near the couloir walls. While waiting our turns to ski, we had time to look out of the shady couloir over snow-draped pines towards more distant peaks. It was very quiet, with just the hiss of departing skis to break the silence. It wasn't like we had a lot of options to discuss.

Everything went well until the final pitch before the couloir dropped over the cliffs at its base, probably a waterfall after a summer rainstorm. Phil had skied off to the right of the chute in order to prospect an exit around the bounding rib. As Alex skied to join him, he slipped off balance, half-tumbled, and lost a ski as he slid. It was one of those dream-like situations where a disaster unfolds before your eyes and

Phil Ingle skiing into the first descent of the couloir on Pic du Jaillon

there is absolutely nothing you can do about it. From above I was about to watch Alex disappear over the edge of the cliff.

Phil, however, with great presence of mind, skied out into the bed of the couloir to intercept Alex, but ended up fielding just the ski, since Alex managed to successfully self-arrest with his ski poles. Phil then moved up to return the ski and support Alex as he got back onto it. In the worst-case scenario, both might have gone over the edge, but later Phil sounded pretty confident that that wouldn't have happened. I guess we all breathed a sigh of relief when Alex was back on ski. Then both of them stepped up to where Phil had previously been waiting.

That hadn't exactly inspired me with confidence, but I was able to ski down to join them without mishap, fully appreciating the seriousness of the position. Some scratchy stepping and sliding contoured around the rib and into the narrow gully beyond. There, our boot tracks showed that in ascent such a traverse had appeared to be a lot more dangerous than it turned out to be in descent. We reached the rib of snowy rock which had been such a struggle to climb, but dropping a little lower put us onto another precarious traverse, skiing out into the snow bowl beyond. From there it was simple enough to ski around to the base of the cliffs and back to our cache of gear.

By then it was late enough for the snow to be refreezing and crusty, making the ski back to Le Coin on the carved-up track a jolting, awkward experience. The exertions of the day had taken their toll, and my skiing showed it.

Compensation after the drive back to Guillestre was found in a bar where several litres of beer and a seemingly endless supply of crisps, olives and peanuts celebrated our achievement.

3

SNOWHOLING IN EARNEST – SWITZERLAND AND JAPAN

More unexpected adventures can creep up on you with a level of seriousness never anticipated.

On a trip to the Bernese Oberland, the team had been mightily impressed at Kleine Scheidegg, gazing up at the north face of the Eiger. Later, at the window of the Eigerwand station on the Jungfraujoch railway, our view down the snow-spattered ice of that north face, sheathed in shadow, prompted a shiver that was more than the chill in the air on the platform.

Suffering badly from the effects of altitude at the top station, we skied raggedly down to the great snow basin of Konkordiaplatz to work on our acclimatisation by spending a couple of nights at the Konkordia hut, and completing a very manageable ski tour on Kranzberg. After route-finding problems on the Grünhorn, a second attempt saw the others turning back, leaving me to solo the peak in deteriorating weather, which was probably about as much adventure as I expected or desired.

We were just a bunch of mates: Jeremy Whitehead, one of the grand old men of British backcountry skiing, and his younger friend, Richard Jones; Aidan Raftery, a member of my local climbing club, and me. In the bad weather that followed my day on the Grünhorn, we resigned ourselves to waiting it out at the hut, but then another team set off for the Hollandia Hut, proposing to exit the Oberland via the

Lötschental if the bad weather continued. The two youngsters in our party, chafing at kicking their heels all day at the hut, jumped at the opportunity for action. Jeremy and I remained doubtful about setting off late in conditions that could worsen, but after lunch, against our better judgement, we agreed to set out and see how it went. After all, it was just a straight route along the Grosser Aletschfirn from one hut to another; what could go wrong?

It went quite well at first, and my misgivings seemed unfounded. Then the weather closed in.

Richard and Aidan seized the initiative with navigation. One skinned ahead while the other kept checking the first was on a straight bearing to the Hollandia Hut some 7 km away. Jeremy and I murmured that it might have been better to take a bearing on something closer, like the buttress beneath point 3178m at 3060m altitude to minimise the chance of error – but, even though we were dubious about the wisdom of the enterprise, we just abdicated responsibility and, in the face of their overwhelming enthusiasm, let Richard and Aidan get on with it. As any landmarks disappeared into the whiteout, I couldn't help feeling that we might be drifting off course. Most people are right-footed so when they think they are walking a straight line they tend to veer to the left, which is why it's possible to walk in a circle when lost in featureless terrain such as deserts and ice caps.

The snowfall increased, and deepened the snowpack substantially the further we travelled. For hours it seemed we were breaking trail through knee-to waist-deep snow and then it was further to go back than to go on. Darkness fell as we pushed on obsessively, convinced the pass was not far away and longing for the comfort and safety of the hut. Aidan tried a tentative whistle but gave up, realising it would be muffled by the wind and snow – and who would be out listening in this weather anyway? All the while we puzzled about the complete absence of any lights shining from the hut.

The fall line of the slope we were climbing had a northerly aspect rather than the easterly one that would have meant that we were climbing up to the Lötschenlücke, where the hut was situated. Jeremy worked out that we must be on the north-facing slopes between the Aletschhorn and the Sattelhorn, which confirmed my worries about our drift left as we had skinned up the glacier. He theorised that traversing right until the slope regained an easterly aspect should put us below the pass, with an easy climb up to the hut. We duly started traversing – but the aspect didn't change. There must have been further to go than he'd thought.

We stopped again to check, with avalanche debris below us and little snowballs trickling down from above in our headtorch beams.

'I don't like this! We need to get off this slope fast!' I shouted above the sound of the storm, and we started to reverse course.

But not fast enough. Before we were quite clear, at the tail, Richard and I were caught in an avalanche. A great wind, laden with snow, flared the torchlight like a halo about my head and swept me off my feet. I swam with the flow, trying to keep my head up and nose and mouth clear, dog-paddling until I came to rest. Immediately both Richard and I began vigorously thrashing about to free ourselves from partial burial before another slide hit us or the snow concretised.

That was enough for me. 'Right. No more struggling in the dark in avalanche terrain. I reckon we should get back down to the flat of the glacier and dig a snowhole. By morning we should at least be able to work out where we are.'

There was no dissent.

Going straight down took us clear of unstable slopes, but I suppose we didn't stop until so well clear that there was no bank of snow in which to excavate a snowhole. That meant digging vertically down about 2 metres into the snow, consuming a lot of time and effort; at least it kept us warm. Next came the tunnelling into the wall of the pit. A small entrance hole was enlarged beyond into a snow cave, pushing out the excavated debris to be shovelled up to those on the surface who in turn deposited it far enough away from the pit to avoid infilling.

Murky route-finding on the way to the Hollandia Hut

We all took turns at different jobs, and after about four hours we had a cramped but adequate refuge. While the others sorted themselves out in the cave, I checked the ski poles were marking our location and semi-roofed the pit with skis; as much to keep them to hand as to keep the snow out. Finally, I wormed my way inside and wriggled into my bivouac bag.

Though cold, our combined body heat kept the temperature above freezing in the constricted space of the snowhole. Unfortunately, it wasn't warm enough to melt the contents of our water bottles as I found when I tipped mine back over my mouth and gained nothing. We catnapped and dozed for about four hours until a faint grey light began to reveal that snow had drifted into the pit, reducing the size of the entrance. It was curious how reluctant everyone was to make a move.

The light strengthened, so I struggled to the entrance and forced my way out through the accumulated snow. An icy blast instantly froze my damp overmitts to a crackling solidity. Clambering out of the pit,

I could see the hut perched to the right of the Lötschenlücke. Snow was still falling, so I quickly marked an arrow with a ski pole in the snow, indicating the direction in case visibility was lost.

'I can see the hut!' I yelled into the pit and one by one the others slowly emerged.

Aidan led off, breaking trail with his new fat skis that didn't tend to sink so deeply beneath the surface as the traditional thinner, lighter skis that the rest of us were using. Even so it took us three hours to cover the kilometre or so to the hut and we all had to take turns to break trail, swapping leader like a team of cyclists. When we were spotted from the hut, a team including some of our friends from the Konkordia hut broke trail down towards us. It was a huge help.

As we reached the hut it became obvious why there had been no lights; great banks of snow had drifted over all the windows. Finally in the refuge of the hut, we spent the rest of the day catching up on eating, drinking and sleeping.

The next day we skied the Ebnefluh in great conditions, but the bad weather was back for a descent from the Lötschental to Blatten, which proved decidedly testing.

***

The Oberland experience was not to be my only brush with adversity in dreadful weather.

Richard and Rhys Nadin were a father and son team that I had climbed with around the south-west of England, and Richard had skied in the Pyrenees with me on several Eagle Ski Club (ESC) tours. They both had experience of skiing in Japan, and offered to jointly run a trip for the ESC programme. Rhys had been married to a Japanese woman, so spoke and read enough of the language to be confident about making all the arrangements.

This would be a first for the club, so it was a largish team of eight that assembled in Sapporo on the island of Hokkaido. All of us had skied with Richard, who had been happy to see us sign up for the tour. One of the team, Almudena Carrasco, had joined the club specifically to go on this trip after meeting Richard in Spain. Her flight from Madrid

Skiing on Mt Yotei

arrived the day after the rest of us, and she was welcomed at the end of our first day skiing at Teine, just 30 minutes from central Sapporo. Teine didn't have lot of lifts, but did have plenty of off-piste options and the promised deep powder through the trees. So far so good.

On 7 February we drove for one and a half hours to Kokusai for what Rhys described as an easy warm-up tour from the top of the lift system. He was so confident that he recommended light, minimalist day-sacks for a skin across the plateau followed by the descent of one or other of the valleys through trees to the road. There it would be easy to get a lift back to the ski station for our drivers to collect the hire cars and pick up the rest of the team. The weather forecast was for temperatures of -8° with windchill reducing that to -20° and some snow in the afternoon. From the car park it looked like a fine day, and that impression continued as we took the cable car up to the top station and began skinning along snowmobile tracks towards the plateau.

On the plateau it was a different story: wild and windswept. We skinned through a weird landscape of birches heavy with encrusted snow. Some of them were bent right over, their topmost branches frozen into the surface below, forming strange arches. Between the trees were wind scoops and sastrugi, twisted into curious snow sculptures by the freeze–thaw cycle and the power of the wind. Cloud and snowfall closed in on us as we struggled through that wind, heads down, hands stiffening with cold. But there was a lot of light in that cloud; I remember the sun hanging above us as a great diffused globe, brightening or dimming as the cloud thinned or thickened. Reaching a col between two insignificant peaks, Rhys decided we should make our first run down into the valley below. If the weather continued bad, we could always continue down to the road.

Excellent powder skiing took us down to a point where fallen trees obstructed the valley bottom, so we skinned back up the flank of a ridge – but no one was keen to climb all the way up into the wind again. There seemed to be some uncertainty about whether we were in the right valley to descend to the road or needed to descend the valley beyond the ridge. When I asked Rhys if I could have a look at the map, I found he only had a ski station sketch map and was struggling because what he could see did not fit what he remembered from other descents in previous years. He thought we should ski down this valley following the drainage and would then be bound to come out at the road.

That seemed fair enough, so we skied off the flank of the ridge and further down through the trees until we reached a pool blocking the way. Steep densely forested slopes surrounded the pool, dropping directly into the water. It looked deep, and I reckoned anyone who slid in on ski stood a good chance of drowning. Rhys had never seen this pool before. The route beyond could easily be blocked by deadfall, and we would have been risking going into the watercourse underlying the snow. We had reached an impasse.

The only other suggestion Rhys could offer was to skin back up the ridge and some way along it, to ski down the other side, which he

thought should take us back to the ski station. The team duly dug out our skins from our rucksacks and fitted them to our skis as best we could as snowfall increased. Deep snow made for tough and time-consuming skinning, all the more difficult as some of us found our damp skins would not stick to the skis in such cold temperatures. Even wrapping duct tape around them did not hold along the length of the ski. Eventually reaching the crest of the ridge, Rhys began following it, but with increasing uncertainty about where to ski down.

The light was beginning to fail, and we needed an exit strategy that would work. Susie Amann and I had both led a number of previous ESC tours, and applied ourselves to the problem. She had a GPS track that would take us back to the top station of the ski lift but we would need to climb up to the plateau again to follow it. That seemed to be our only assured way out of the situation, but skinning through deep snow continued to be time-consuming and sapped our energy despite taking turns to break trail.

The failing light was making it obvious that we weren't going to get back to the top station in daylight. We stopped to take stock.

'Everyone okay?' There were affirmative noises, or at least no one demurred. 'There's still a good way to the GPS track,' Susie began, 'and most of us haven't got head-torches, so we can't go on all night. I think we should dig a snowhole.'

'To be honest,' I said, 'I'm doubtful about climbing up into the wind on that plateau in any case. We're all tired, hungry and cold, and it would be easy for someone to become hypothermic. But we *could* traverse along the slopes below the edge of the plateau – parallel with the GPS track as you have it on your display, but out of the wind.'

'And the snowhole?'

'I'm reluctant to dig a snowhole too soon. We're keeping warm by keeping moving. People get cold standing around while a snowhole is being dug, even taking turns to work at it, and I've not seen a good depth of snow yet to dig into on this ridge. The nearer we are to the lift station the closer we are to safety or any rescue party.'

'Okay, but I've a feeling a snowhole is inevitable.'

'Yes, I think you're right. Sooner or later. I'm looking out for a suitable spot.'

Shortly afterwards I noticed a wide break going down through the trees in the dusk, and for a moment thought it might be a way back to the piste; but Rhys didn't recognise it, and I had to accept that we could follow it only to find our way blocked by forest and insufficient or unsuitable snow for a snowhole. We'd be safer to stick with shadowing the GPS track.

It was close to full dark when I called a halt at a large tree.

'Going on is going to be risky when people can't see where they're going.' Susie was right on the money. 'We should dig a snowhole.'

'Yep. We should, and there's a windscoop just below this tree that might be just right. I'll go take a look.'

Almudena spoke good English one-to-one, but was finding it hard to follow what was going on in our clipped exchanges with the wind whipping our words away. This was her first day skiing with the ESC, and she had no idea what was going on. Susie had been conversing with her in Spanish, so Almudena asked her what we were doing, and Susie explained we would be spending the night in a hole in the snow. Almudena is one of the toughest women I've known and I've heard her tell this story several times since; at this point she always adds, '… and I didn't cry!'

Richard Handy and I started in on the job, digging horizontally into the snowbank of the windscoop while the others cleared the snow we had excavated and shovelled out through the entrance tunnel. In 40 minutes we had a snowhole spacious enough for eight people. Fortunately, some of us had not left all our emergency gear behind. One four-person bivouac sack was rigged with ski poles to block off the entrance from intrusive wind gusts, while two more were shared between the team. Sitting on our rucksacks, feet in bivouac bags, we spent 13 hours wiggling toes, shifting sore bums and cold backs to different positions and intermittently shivering, but for the most part the temperature was warmed above freezing level by our body heat contained in the snow cave. By the light of Kerstin's phone-torch, for an astonishing number of hours, we snoozed, woke up, chilled and rewarmed, shadow-boxed and told stories until a grey dawn gathered enough light for us to move out into the bitter cold.

Driving spindrift had reduced visibility, but in daylight it was possible to work out a good skinning line up onto the plateau and to follow our GPS track. The weather cleared to hard bright sunlight

On the plateau returning to Kokusai, Day Two

wielded bladelike by wind and cloud as we skinned through a stunted, sparse woodland of dwarf birch trees with snow plastered against their trunks. Every twig was encrusted with sparkling ice, like Christmas decorations.

Back at the top station of the gondola, as the engines turned the great cables, it was another world. One run down the piste took us to the restaurant for a snack and drink before driving back to the hotel where none of us wanted anything more than to catch up on our sleep. Like little children, we escaped the aftermath of a harrowing experience by lapsing into unconsciousness.

Fortunately, despite continuing unsettled weather, we had some fine days skiing deep powder on the rest of the trip.

***

None of us expected those adventures. They just crept up on us; 'incident creep' when a number of small incidents accumulate to deliver a difficult situation, an unexpected adventure. Some might regard those events as epics, but I don't think so. An epic is a disaster averted far more narrowly.

Guidelines

- an *adventure* is when you go to the pub afterwards and talk about it;
- an *epic* is when you go to the pub afterwards and don't want to talk about it;
- a *disaster* is when you don't get to the pub.

If the weather had not improved and we had been forced to stay in the snowholes, if one of us had succumbed to hypothermia or been injured in an avalanche, then the adventure could have become an epic, perhaps even a disaster. Some bad judgement calls were made, and some good ones. We had the skills to survive, and we were lucky.

An adventure can be looked back on with a positive feeling about it. There was adversity but it was overcome; the mistakes were understandable; the remedial strategies worked; we learnt from the experience. But I have to qualify that. After my first night in a snowhole I told myself that I would never allow that to happen again, yet it did. There are no guarantees with adventures.

HUT-TO-HUT ADVENTUROUS JOURNEYS

Whilst day tours can result in some memorable adventures, there is no doubt that they are usually less committing than hut-to-hut tours. Even if a week of day tours is planned, it's generally possible to take a day or two off, if fitness, injury or weather are likely to cause problems. If a day tour proves to be more dangerous or demanding than expected, the roadhead and a warm bed are likely to be nearby.

Hut-to-hut tours tend to follow more remote routes across a series of passes, and, whilst there are often escape routes, those may involve their own difficulties. The word 'hut' or 'hutte,' used in English and German, indicates the basic nature of the shelter on offer, and the Latinate 'refuge', 'refugio' or 'rifugio' indicates the function of these mountain retreats, which can be life-savers in the conditions experienced on high mountains.

Planning a route linking huts needs to include contingency planning in case it turns out that a pass is impassable owing to avalanche risk, for example, and the team is put under additional pressure by day after day of exertion and nervous tension. Some people don't react well to those demands, whilst others relish the challenge. Co-operation, not competition, is the key to success, and it's interesting to see how members of a team grow into the role, or not. One of the tests can be how they respond to another member having difficulties; are they helpful or dismissive? Is this a team player? The last skier you want in a team is the one that hurtles down a crowded piste, thinking he's a downhill racer (it's usually but not exclusively a 'he') without the slightest consideration for other skiers he may collide with.

A note on maps

Most of these routes are too long for suitably detailed maps to be printed in this book. Instead, I have included links to internet sources which will allow you to zoom in and out on maps for the degree of detail you require to track the features of the routes described. These links are found at the end of each chapter. The exception is the Silvretta tour, where just two huts were used as bases for day tours.

4

THE HAUTE ROUTE

This must be the most famous ski tour in the world, perhaps because it links the two premier alpine centres of Chamonix and Zermatt, extending to Saas Fee if desired. With a length of nearly 90 miles and crossing more than 20 glaciers it has a total ascent and descent that approximates to that of Everest from sea level! But it is not just a ski-mountaineering challenge; it is a route through some of the finest mountain scenery in the world in the ski tracks of the earliest pioneers.

Initially developed as a summer route on foot by British alpinists, the first detailed description appeared in the forerunner to the *Alpine Club Journal,* 'Peaks, Passes and Glaciers' of 1862. At the start of the 20th century, ski-mountaineering pioneers such as Dr Hebling and Dr Payot were seeking to complete a ski route as directly as possible, but it was not until 1911 that the connection from Bourg St Pierre over the Plateau du Couloir and Col du Sonadon, descending the Mt Durand Glacier to Chanrion, was made by Marcel Kurz, Professor Roget and guides. The Classic Haute Route was complete, and it is worth noting that it was not until 1926 that the easier Verbier variation was skied from the Mont Fort Hut over the Rosablanche to the Dix Hut.

In his seminal work, *Ski Mountaineering,* Peter Cliff comments:

We should not forget all the hard work of the early pioneers in finding a way round the south side of the Grand Combin, that is the Haute Route. If you find an easy option which avoids the main difficulties, you may have some good ski mountaineering and you may have a nice time but you will not have done the Haute Route.

That was a challenge hard to ignore.

Arriving in Chamonix, my team made straight for the Météo notice-board, across the road from the church, where a forecast of *'beau temps'* for the next five days was greeted with a mixture of excitement and incredulity. If we hadn't been suffering from a kind of jetlag after driving all night from Calais, an afternoon ascent to the Argentière Refuge would have given us a flying start to our route, but instead the team mellowed out in the Easter sunshine with a couple of beers at a quiet street café. Although Denis, Ralph and I were all teachers, alpinists and skiers of long standing, we were relatively new to ski-touring. There had been some dabbling at day tours in Chamonix the year before, but we'd recognised that hut-to-hut touring was far more challenging. So, with an Easter break to fill, we decided to go for the Haute Route from Chamonix to Zermatt as our first hut-to-hut tour. We all expected an adventure!

Like good alpinists, we phoned the Argentière Refuge, but with no response, so next morning, with a tight schedule of just over a week, parked at the Grand Montets *téléphérique,* sorted out our packs and skis, and bought tickets to the top. When we reached the Lognan halfway station, the top section of the lift was closed owing to high winds. After waiting for an hour with no signs of progress and fruitlessly phoning the Argentière Hut yet again, Ralph queried, 'Time for a drink?' There was no argument, but just as we sat down, he spotted the first cabin going up to the top station. Downing our beers, we dashed back to find ourselves at the end of a brand-new queue, which delayed us a further hour and left us feeling tense and angry. Perhaps we were still a little jet-lagged. In retrospect we should probably have bought a day ticket to ski until late afternoon and then gone over to the hut, but our anxieties about the weather and securing accommodation at the hut had ruled that out.

As we finally stepped out on the snow at the top station, a cold wind cut at us, but it felt good to be skiing down the glacier away from the crowds, with the Aiguilles Chardonnet and Argentière towering splendidly above us and flanking the notch of the Col du Chardonnet, which was to be our first objective next morning. Then patches of dense cloud blew in, to take visibility down to nothing. In the whiteout there was absolutely nothing to distinguish between sky, snow and the cloud between; we were skiing by the feel of the unseen snow beneath our skis. It felt vaguely like flying. Then the cloud would clear and each of us tried to pick a line between the crevasses and ski it before the next cloud rolled in. These were difficult conditions in which to keep one's balance, not helped by the 13 kg rucksacks on our backs. Any miscalculation was punished unmercifully by the extra weight, and in an area of hidden crevasses we were all anxious not to fall heavily.

On the Argentière Glacier, an occasional skier whizzed past us in the opposite direction, heading back to the pistes, as we stuck skins onto our skis and began climbing up to the hut. Behind us the whoops of excitement from a party that had traversed from the Grands Montets to ski down the couloir to the left of the Pyramide d'Argentière faded into the distance. The weather was clearing and we reached the hut with only one awkward icy section that required careful edging above a rocky drop. The hut was wardened, which was a relief. The staff had been setting the hut up for opening that day, and just couldn't be bothered to answer the phone. Very French! Sitting in the sunshine outside the hut, I was impressed by the Argentière Wall opposite, in winter raiment. The north faces of the Verte, Droites and Courtes were stark white rather than blackened with summer stone-fall, but there was plenty of windswept ice, and it looked damned cold up there.

Leaving the Argentière Refuge at first light, side-slipping gingerly down an exposed icy traverse, I noticed from the tracks that whoever had started before us had opted to walk in crampons, but we were soon skiing easily down the Argentière Glacier to its junction with the Glacier du Chardonnet. At a little spur on the true left bank of that glacier, we found vestigial tracks leading up – but Denis also found that he'd left his sweater at the hut. Dumping his rucksack, he skinned back up the glacier to collect it. Ralph and I finished fixing our skins and added another fleece, but still felt cold. I started up a little way, adjusted my boots, felt colder, then, little by little, went up a bit further. Just before we would have lost sight of his rucksack behind the convexity of the slope we were climbing, Denis reappeared and hurriedly got stuck in to catching up with us.

After zigzagging steeply up the initial slopes, we emerged onto a snowfield that rose more steadily to a final step at the Col du Chardonnet 3323m. Just two days out from England, the altitude was beginning to affect us; each of us was forced to slump over our ski poles, gasping for breath, at one time or another. The crest of the col was icy snow, chilled by a bitter wind that hit us like a slap in the face as we went over the top. Ahead, one party was in the process of abseiling down from the col, while another waited to rig their abseil. We ducked back into the lee of the col to wait. Once they were clear, Denis opted to down-climb, but Ralph and I preferred the security of roping down. A few metres below the crest the ice petered out, and the angle and quality of the snow was certainly skiable (typical steep couloir skiing) but none of us had the confidence to ski it with heavy sacks. As we reached a more reasonable angle and were stepping into our bindings again, a party with tiny French day-sacks did ski down from the crest, but one had the good grace to say that it had been more like a barely controlled fall, 'with plenty of bottom-braking' he said, slapping his backside.

Skinning up from the Argentière Glacier towards the Aiguille du Chardonnet

A short slope led to a long gentle traverse in full sun with tremendous views of the north face of the Aiguille d'Argentière and across the Glacier de Saleina towards the Grand Combin, with the Wiesshorn and Dent Blanche in the distance. Some poling was necessary across flattish sections until we shot around a snow spur at the foot of the Grande Fourche to reach the start of the climb to the Fenêtre du Saleina. Skins went on again, and we climbed steadily in the tracks of those before us until the final steep section was reached. Strenuous

Skinning towards the Col du Chardonnet

zigzagging had suited some, but we opted to take our skis off and boot up direct, kicking steps, which we reckoned would save time on the steepest ground. Altitude kicked in at about the same time, and again there was lots of heavy breathing as headaches gathered behind the eyes. Reaching 3261m at the top, I looked back through the enclosing walls of the pass which formed a perfect frame for a view of the Grand Lui beyond.

When Ralph and Denis arrived, there was some argument about whether to go on to Champex, skiing the Val d'Arpette that afternoon, or to stay overnight at the Trient Hut as planned. We'd made good time, and it's not unusual for an acclimatised party of good skiers in good conditions to reach Champex from the Grand Montets in a day; but we didn't know what accommodation would be available in Champex, and Denis and I both felt that another night at altitude would be good for our acclimatisation. So we stayed high, and that afternoon soaked up the sunshine and admired the panorama from the terrace of the Refuge de Trient at 3170m. The pinnacled ridge of the Aiguilles Dorées looked particularly impressive, and Denis and I both made a mental note to climb it, though it would be more than a year before we did so.

The clocks went back that night, so we lost an hour's sleep but started early enough, at 7.30 am. The angle of the glacier was easy, but snow conditions were difficult, varying from hard névé to breakable crust, which would suddenly catch us out, though we kept our speed down to avoid falls. Schussing on to a rounded spur on the right of the glacier to traverse over to the Fenêtre du Chamois, Denis and I left our rucksacks and skis to scramble up and take a look over the edge. The other side was steep and rocky but with more snow the angle would be skiable. Tracks showed someone had stepped down on ski, probably also on abseil, to ski off below the rocks. That didn't look much fun to either of us. We climbed back to our skis to follow the guidebook's recommendation to ski steeply down to the Trient Glacier and around to the Col des Ecandies. This descent was certainly steep. Ralph stared down at it uncertainly, and said, 'I don't think I can ski that.'

'Oh, come on,' Denis laughed, 'You can sideslip down most stuff off-vertical.'

'Take your time, and you'll be fine,' I suggested.

He did and he was.

Shaded from the sun, the snow quality was good and the run proved to be no more difficult than an unpisted black run in a resort but really exhilarating despite the weight of our rucksacks.

As I reached the right turn around the base of the enclosing spur, I realised why I'd seen people stop there; a crevasse much like a bergschrund ran right across the slope, widening from right to left and ending in a jumble of collapsed seracs. This must be the crevasse that had rendered the route impassable in the past and clearly might do so in future. A fall at the wrong point here could be disastrous. Traversing the upper lip of the crevasse to its narrowest point, I turned, crossing the crevasse with a jump, then quickly turned again on the steep slope below to put me on line for the traverse to the col. Waiting for Denis

and Ralph to follow, I was able to take a couple of photos, and fortunately nothing dramatic befell them. We traversed easily to the col and climbed the short rocky step to the crest with our skis over our shoulders.

Back in the sun, though the slope below was not technical, the snow was variable, causing a few tumbles amongst the parties ahead of us. By traversing out to the left I found a steep little run on perfect icy névé, which took me down to the long traverse out to the right on heavy snow. By keeping high on the traverse, I was able to find further steep runs on better snow using short radius turns, though always in danger of being taken by surprise by a change in snow quality. In the event, this happened to Ralph and to me; I suddenly found myself breaking through crust at speed and managed a head-plant that put my glasses round my neck and left my face ice-scratched, whilst Ralph was clouted by his skis in a fall that broke his sun-glasses, grazed his nose and blacked his eye. He demanded that I take a photo with his camera to record the damage.

Funnelling down into the valley bottom, we found the snow improved on much-skied tracks, and then a snow-covered road that offered a long, thigh-cramping schuss to the Auberge d'Arpette at the summer roadhead. There I ordered some celebratory beers and we took a well-deserved rest in the sunshine. Looking back up the valley, the Col des Ecandies seemed a very long way off.

The road beyond was snowed up for most of its length, lying in the shade of trees, so that we were able to ski to within 100m of Champex with only a couple of places where we needed to step carefully across thawed-out sections. At Champex we reached the supermarket in time to buy bread, cheese and more beer for an improvised lunch beside the still-frozen lake, but the complications of a Sunday bus timetable meant that we had to take a taxi to Bourg St Pierre.

By that time, we were conscious of the need to save at least a day on the route if we were to stand a chance of finishing in good weather, and had discussed various ways of combining sections of the route to do so. In the taxi we revisited these discussions, animated by the beers consumed on nearly empty stomachs. The taxi-driver volunteered to

Traversing to the Col des Ecandies

drive us up the road as far as the snowline if we decided to go all the way to the Valsorey Hut that day, so that's what we did. It was the right decision at the time, but all of us had cause to regret it later. At 2.30 pm, having been dropped off on the road up the Valsorey Valley, where it was well and truly blocked with snow, we set out on a five-hour hut walk.

We started up a faint track by a stream until I tired of carrying skis and suggested crossing the stream and skinning up the snow on the shady bank opposite. This went well until we came to a little dam with avalanche debris piled up behind it. Some skiers were coming down this, and reached us to say that it wasn't easy but was a quick way up. A tricky traverse on snowy branches over a deep pool turned Ralph back and prompted Denis to take off his skis, but I reasoned that if the French team had skied down, then I should be able to skin up, and did so. The avalanche debris was steep and awkward – so awkward that despite my optimism I had to take off my skis eventually and force a way up through tangled branches to follow Denis out onto a less inclined part of the valley. Tired and clumsy, neither of us could be bothered to consult the map or altimeter, and so had no real idea of our exact location as we followed the tracks upwards.

Denis and I crossed back left to avoid cliffs, and Ralph caught us up, having kept to what had turned out to be a good track. I thought I could see the hut in the distance but suddenly reached a fork in the track and realised that we were a lot lower than I'd surmised; the hut in front of us was the Velan Hut, not the Valsorey. Disappointed but determined, we slogged on in full afternoon sun up the Valsorey Gorge, a narrow defile blocked with huge snowed-up boulders. A twisting track wound steeply between them, and in places the muffled roar of water thundered eerily beneath the snow under our skis.

Nearing the top of the gorge, we found that the angle eased, and when we climbed out of the valley to the left, the Valsorey Hut finally appeared in the distance, at the head of a daunting slope. Thankfully, it was 6 pm and some of the heat had abated, as the avalanche danger from that slope was notorious enough to be mentioned in the guidebook. A little breeze blew up, easing our suffering as we toiled up that last 400m. Arriving at 7.30 pm, we quickly ordered a meal while they were still serving, although as it turned out both Ralph and Denis felt too ill to eat theirs; a nasty combination of exhaustion and the effects of altitude.

From the Valsorey Hut next morning we cramponed up rocky slopes too steep to skin, using well-kicked snow steps icy enough to make us take extra care in the pre-dawn cold. The moon had rendered headtorches redundant, casting our shadows onto the crusted snow as we left the hut, and as we climbed the chill dawn light gradually added colour to the scene. At 3664m the Plateau de Couloir was our highest pass, and several people in other parties were having a hard time on the ascent. I felt well enough acclimatised to be climbing easily, reaching the pass before the sun.

There was a little bivouac hut on this spur of the Grand Combin, and tracks showed that previous parties had climbed up onto the summit ridge from this point. It's an impressive place for a bivouac, perched in a red steel box amidst spectacular scenery. The weather was perfectly clear, but a cold wind threatened to ice up any moisture on the skis. It was too cold to hang around.

Skiing across to the Col du Sonadon involved a steep traverse and long schuss on heavy snow before skinning up to the col itself, where we took a first snack stop. The view back towards Mont Blanc in the crystal-clear atmosphere reminded us how far we had travelled. Weaving down around the ice cliffs of the Mt Durand Glacier, first left, then right, along a pronounced shelf above an icefall, was complicated enough for us to be very glad that the visibility was so good. A traverse off to the right to avoid crevasses then required the refitting of skins to climb up a short section and take another break on a little spur. Snow conditions from there down to the junction with the Otemma Glacier were variable and difficult; mostly heavy and requiring controlled balance skiing, but with occasional strips of icier snow that provided enjoyable steep little runs.

We had speculated about going on up the Otemma Glacier to miss out the Chanrion Hut and reach the Vignettes Hut in a day, but by then it was much too hot, and we were still tired from our efforts of the previous day. During the discussion, all three of us confessed to a sneaking desire to traverse the Pigne d'Arolla on the way to the Vignettes Hut. The description sounded far more interesting than flogging up the Otemma Glacier.

Even the 200m up to the Chanrion Hut proved hard enough in the heat, and we were pleased to arrive and unwind in the sunshine.

Denis and I took full advantage of the water available at this altitude, just 2462m, taking turns at the overflow pipe from the water trough for a memorable washdown, barefoot in the snow. All of us washed four days' sweat out of at least some of our clothes, drying them easily as we sunbathed, shirtless, on the terrace. This was often the most relaxing part of the day; nights tended to be restless, disturbed by people snoring or coughing and often hot and stuffy. This hut wasn't crowded, though, and after a satisfying meal of chamois steak and mash, I managed to catch up on some really deep sleep, only once aware of Denis's uncharacteristic snores. In the

Skiing down the Val d'Arpette to Champex

morning he was complaining of chest pains and coughing up phlegm, which was worrying, but at least Ralph's swollen eye had gone down, though still bruised. Overall, the crux section of the route had been kind to us.

Rising at 5.45 am, we breakfasted on four-day-old bread and jam brought with us in case the Chanrion Hut had been unwardened. There had been a warning in the guidebook that that might be the case, and it was certainly quieter than other huts. The guardian wasn't particularly happy about it, but at least he sold us hot drinks, and from our point of view it lightened our loads.

The day dawned fine and clear, so there was nothing to stop us going over the Pigne d'Arolla. One party had already set out, and following their tracks I could see the imprints of the teeth of their harscheisen punched into the ice beneath my skis, but it was not until I was overtaken by a German party, similarly equipped, as I struggled to edge on particularly hard ice, that I appreciated their foresight, stopped, and fixed

On the Plateau du Couloir

my own. Once established on the gently rising Glacier du Brenay, however, harscheisen caused unnecessary drag, so I quickly returned them to the rucksack and skinned up the 500m to the icefall at half height.

There, ice axes and crampons came out and, carrying skis, a further 200m were climbed to the left of the broken icefall. The zigzag crampon track scratched across the face of the ice slope mounted out of the cold shadow of the lower glacier past angular blue seracs into the sun. At the top, a German woman was too shattered by the effort and tension to take off her crampons, and just sat on her rucksack, 'spaced out', until one of her friends removed them for her.

Above the icefall, the glacier rose steadily for another 500m to the summit of the Pigne d'Arolla at 3796m; quite an effort in full sun, though a sharp wind blew straight into our faces at times to cool us. Denis had been coughing, and despite me dropping the pace I think he'd still found it tough. When we reached the saddle above the east face, between the main summit and a subsidiary peak to the south, he left his rucksack to make the final ascent unencumbered. There was faint high cirrus lacing the sky, but the views from the summit were superb, back towards the distant Mont Blanc massif and forward to the huge teeth of the Zermatt giants, the Dent d'Herens and Matterhorn to the right, and the Dent Blanche, Zinalrothorn and Wiesshorn ranging to the left.

On the summit we met several people, including some not seen since Champex. A group of Spaniards told us that they had taken a bus to Verbier, making their way from there to the Dix Hut, and were now crossing the Pigne d'Arolla to rejoin the Haute Route at the Vignettes Hut. This easier variation seemed to be quite popular, and it was clear that they regarded the Classic Haute Route from the Valsorey Hut to the Chanrion as a much more serious undertaking. I think all of my team were glad to have done it and to have avoided the tedious trudge up the Otemma Glacier by reaching this summit, the highest point of the tour.

Skiing down from the summit was a dream of speed, rhythm and good snow. By then we were all well-used to skiing with rucksacks which had grown lighter by the day as we consumed our lunch rations and drinks. Pure enjoyment came to an end below some ice cliffs at a slope of steep, slushy snow cut by a crevasse. A smoothed ski track skirted above the crevasse but required a precise turn under ice cliffs to cross at its narrowest point; fluff the turn and you could bounce off the ice wall into the crevasse. Everyone skied it slowly and carefully before schussing across to the little ridge that led to the Vignettes Hut and provided a last few minutes of excitement. It was necessary to ski onto a narrow tongue of snow above a big drop, edge carefully up to the crest of the ridge, stepping over rocks, then traverse along icy tracks above another big drop on the other side. It was okay if you didn't look down.

The Vignettes Hut is in an amazing location, perched on the edge of a cliff, and for that reason has no terrace from which to enjoy the sun, just a gangway over the void, leading to a traditional long-drop toilet. We managed to sort out some rocky perches which were safe enough to dry out our boots in the sunshine, then went in to begin the serious business of rehydration. A variety of drinks from cuppasoups to mint tea were brewed, whilst the warden intermittently opened a window to shovel banked snow directly into huge vessels heating on the massive stove.

Skiing off the Pigne d'Arolla to the Vignettes Hut

We were drawn into conversation with an American who had the disconcerting habit of blowing his nose on any convenient article of his expensive Patagonia clothing. He and his Swedish girlfriend had reached here from Verbier on telemark skis, but had lost one of their team who had to be helicoptered off with a smashed knee. The American was convinced the lightness of telemark skis was what they needed for such a long route, but his girlfriend seemed more doubtful and we never heard the injured guy's opinion.

To our surprise Denis and I recognised the Zermatt guide, Victor Imboden, whom Denis and I had met on the Alphubel–Täschhorn–Dom traverse the previous summer. At the Mischabeljoch bivouac hut, he had been desperately trying to call in a helicopter to assist in the rescue of two of his more experienced clients who had been roped together descending the north ridge of the Alphubel, when they slipped and slid into a crevasse. He was more cheerful on this occasion, and maintained that a few years ago he had completed the Haute Route nine times in a season; Zermatt to Chamonix, change clothes, Chamonix to Zermatt, and so on.

The hut was crowded with day trippers from Arolla, up to do the Pigne d'Arolla or just to have a night at the hut. A tall, loose-limbed Spanish girl was in tears because her eye had closed up after a fall on the descent from the Pigne d'Arolla. A German woman was outside the hut, having a heated argument over a two-way radio, which seemed to concern a missing couple. At 2 am, when I cautiously traversed icy planks above the void to the toilet, she was still there but silent. One group was celebrating a birthday and eventually stumbled to their beds uncaring of anyone or anything else. Here we had our only dubious meal; stuffed chicken joints that appeared distinctly pink and thoroughly upset my stomach that night and the following morning.

During the ascent of the Pigne d'Arolla there had been some nervousness about the weather, since that had been the last day forecast to be good. With only one more day to reach Zermatt it was a relief to note the clear sky overnight as that day was a big one – 19 miles, three cols over 3000m, more than 1000m of ascent – and we needed to be over the last col by midday in order to have reasonable snow conditions for the descent of the Stockji Glacier. The guidebook recommended leaving the hut at 3 or 4 am, but breakfast wasn't served until 5 am and we finally left at 6.

I'd had to force breakfast down and Denis was still coughing as we skied off the little ridge on a fast traverse by the light of headtorches towards Petit Mont Collon before bearing left towards Col de l'Evêque. It was a bit like doing 70 mph down a dark motorway with no headlights.

Tricky kick-turns on the Col du Mont Brulé

Reaching the lowest point as the sun began to rise into an overcast sky, we fumbled the skins on with numb fingers and then made good time winding around crevasses to the crest of Col de l'Evêque. It was a well-paced, gradual climb, but cold even in the sunlight as we stripped skins at the pass. The weather was holding.

A pleasant ski descent on good snow followed, which steepened as we kept to the right of the Glacier d'Arolla before schussing out to the start of the rise to the Col du Mont Brulé. This long ascent remained in the shadow of the ridge, climbing gradually until the last icy steepening to the crest of the col. Some walked this final pitch in crampons, others fitted harscheisen, but it looked like a well-skinned track to me, and using harscheisen meant losing the benefit of the step on the binding, so I pushed on without them. There were some very technical kick-turns overcome by careful edging, acutely aware of the drop beneath. My stomach had settled down by then, and Denis had been keeping up well although he looked a bit rough; I suppose we were both absorbed in the business of climbing. The rocks at the head of the pass were bright with sunshine, and reaching them we were greeted by the bulking presence of the Dent d'Herens ahead with the Matterhorn peering over its shoulder.

Skiing an easy traverse line left around the head of the Haute Glacier de Tsa de Tsan put us onto a more or less direct ascent to the Col de Valpelline, at 3568m the highest of the three passes. With skins on we slogged up the 400m to the pass in full sunshine, though the few wisps of cloud which had hung about since first light began thickening, and even threw an odd patch of obscurity across the face of the sun. It was a long way. As I climbed, I felt an increasing pain from my ankle but could see nothing obviously wrong so ignored it, to my cost, in the obsessive rhythm of skinning. Reaching the head of the col by 11.30 am, we were treated to better views of the Dent d'Herens and the Matterhorn, and stopped to take photos, despite the cold, as increasing high cloud diminished the heat from the sun.

There were still good snow conditions on the Stockji Glacier as we skied down steep slopes between seracs, but by this time my ankle was giving me hell; I discovered that one of the plastic flaps on the boot had been digging into the joint. All I could do to control the pain was keep the speed down and anticipate any stressing of the area as I

Skiing down the Stockji Glacier to Zermatt

skied, but Denis was looking a lot more cheerful, and we all knew that now the odds were stacked in our favour. We swung widely right, then down a steep slushy slope onto the Tiefmattengletscher to weave back left avoiding ice cliffs and crevasses. Then, keeping high for the best snow, we skied back right on long traverses and schusses under the foreshortened north face of the Matterhorn, where snowed-up seracs were frozen into immobility and, looking back, we saw a fringe of ice appearing above ice-scoured rock. Eventually coming out on the piste at Stafelalp, we ducked into a skiers' restaurant to celebrate with some expensive beers and recognition as *Haute Routiers*, basking in cloud-filtered sunshine while the Matterhorn's north face grew colder and darker above.

An unpleasantly slushy piste traversed along the valley to Furri, where a short walk led to the cableway down to Zermatt. Damp slabs of soil were emerging from under the snow, with strange smells of growth and decay in the weak spring sunshine after so much time spent with the dead purity of snow. As we walked the pavements of Zermatt to the Hotel Bahnhof, the first few big drops of rain clipped us, and by the time we had settled into the attic the streets were soaked.

That night brought fine snow and warm cloud, which continued for most of the following day. The weather forecast remained unsettled, so we gave up any idea of continuing to Saas Fee or even the hope of a day skiing fresh snow; the avalanche risk would be too great. Our friend Carol had driven over in my car to take us back to Chamonix, and next day that's exactly what we did, descending winding roads out of the snow into rain.

****

To follow this route there are two useful resources:

High altitude ski tour: Haute Route from Argentière to Zermatt • Long ... (outdooractive.com) (see Maps & QR Codes p.228) This route is not exactly the Classic Haute Route. It avoids the Col du Chardonnet and diverts to an Italian Hut instead of traversing the Pigne D'Arolla or Otemma Glacier to the Vignettes Hut, as well as including an unnecessary night at the Schönbiel Hut. However, the computerised maps allow the reader to zoom in to track both routes.

Haute Route Map [Chamonix to Zermatt] (natgeomaps.com) is a booklet and map guide that would be useful in the field.

5

SLEDS IN THE SILVRETTA

For early British alpinists the journey to the Alps took days. Steamers from Dover delivered them to Calais, and steam trains thence through France – perhaps stopping off to visit an acquaintance in Paris as Whymper did in 1860 – then on to Switzerland, where rail would give way to travel by horse-drawn chaise and, higher up, by mule or on foot until climbing could actually begin. By 2001 regular flights combined with the excellent Swiss rail network had made possible raids of less than a week into the mountains, snatching adventures from busy work schedules.

Within 24 hours from home our team of four was settled into Klosters youth hostel and packed for the climb to the Chamanna Tuoi Hut next day. Jeff and I had climbed together in the Alps and made trips to the Bernese Oberland to climb 4000m peaks on ski whilst I'd met Simon through the Eagle Ski Club. Simon now had designs on Alaskan objectives, so intended to test a new haul system for sledges on this trip, bringing along his friend David. Limited time and an unsettled long-range weather forecast had meant that we'd decided to visit only two huts, making day tours from each. From both huts it was possible to reach the valley and reconnect with the railway in just a few hours if the weather turned really nasty.

Next morning, a short train journey took us to Guarda, where we were soon skinning up a good track in sunny weather that progressively became cloudier as we climbed. The impression that this track was somehow 'pisted' was confirmed when a mini rat-track supplying the hut descended to meet us en route. Simon was conscious that he presented an unusual sight, towing his pulk, but he needn't have worried. A sizeable dogsled stood outside the hut, with the dog-team dug into snug straw-filled snowholes, their entrances sheltered by one wall of the hut. There was a long chain attached to steel stake hammered into the snow at one end of the open space between the hut wall and the snowholes, and the dogs were individually tethered to it. They didn't look much like the sled dogs – big hairy beasts – that I'd seen before. These were smaller, and each of them wore a neat padded coat. To the normal scent of woodsmoke on the air when approaching a hut was now added a rank smell of wet dog.

'We're heading for Andermatt, on a 700km traverse of the range,' one of the dog mushers told us, surrounded by broadcast-quality video equipment. Swiss TV was there in force, with a helicopter clattering overhead for aerial shots of the dogs. The cameraman, however, appeared to be more interested in Simon, stripped down to his string vest and underpants to keep cool as he'd climbed, arriving at the hut in light snowfall with his pulk. As the chopper hovered above, I had to admit he was an unusual sight.

A struggling dog-team taking a bend in the trail

Once we'd sorted out our kit, the others headed off into the increasing snowfall for a late afternoon practice skin and ski, but I was more interested in people-watching. Some of the media folk looked as though they had never been near a hut before, but were very fashionable and interacted within an obvious hierarchical framework.

In a bitterly cold, clear morning, the dogs were away earlier than us, but were having a desperate time in soft deep snow on the climb up to Plan Rai. Following the zigzag tracks of the dogs, we took the opportunity to appreciate the position of the hut under the spectacular south-east face of Piz Buin, our target for the day. We soon caught up with the sled as the dog-team rested, then the dogs in turn overtook us on ascending gentler slopes, but we caught up again at the steeper pass out of Plan Rai. On more rolling ground, they had the edge, but as soon as the terrain steepened, dogs and sledders had to put in an enormous amount of effort, which forced them to take more breaks for recovery. The Alps are not natural dog-sledding territory.

It's not every day that there's a chance to be seen ski-touring on Swiss TV, so when the dog-team and its entourage headed off towards the Silvrettapass, it was with some regrets that we left them, to skin more steeply up to the Fuorcla del Cunfin, a notch on the ridge to the north. Beyond was the head of the Ochsentaler glacier with Piz Buin standing clear on the other side of it. Dots of climbers from the closer Wiesbadener Hut were already nearing the summit. On the skin across to the peak we lost any anxiety about travelling in-line with any hidden crevasses, as the depth of snow became obvious. It was possible to reach the rocks of the north-east ridge before having to leave our skis.

Good bucket steps were softening in the sun or being smashed by early birds descending, but we made good time, soloing increasingly mixed ground to an awkward little traverse and short couloir, protected by bolts in the exposed rock of its walls. I was lucky enough to be ahead of some guided parties, which proceeded to festoon this area with ropes and hold up the others behind them. Above, easy slopes of snow and scree led to an airy summit with a huge cross at 3312m.

It was quiet on the top until roped parties arrived, casually crowding onto the small summit platform, confident in the misplaced belief that

their ropes would prevent them from being pushed off. I left the mêlée to meet Jeff, Simon and David arriving at the final step, then descended the rest of the ridge to get back to the skis with enough time for a leisurely lunch. Jeff arrived there next, and he and I became thoroughly chilled while waiting, so as soon as Simon and David neared us Jeff and I took off down the steep powder snow beneath, schussing halfway across the head of the Ochsentaler Glacier before losing momentum and needing to fix skins again.

From the Fuorcla del Cunfin it was a straightforward ski back to the hut, but the snow had turned heavy in afternoon sunshine. It was my first skiing of the season, and I soon regretted missing out on a piste day at a nearby ski resort that would have helped refresh my skills. Jeff was also suffering and David and Simon, telemarking stylishly, soon passed us as we grumbled together about our clumsy efforts. It had been a long day.

Skinning is fine, just a sort of elegant walking, but the first ski run of the season on unpisted snow after a hard climb and months without practice is always challenging, as was the snowfall the following morning. Something of a clearance at 10 am started some parties up the hill. and we headed tentatively for the Jamspitz, although it wasn't long before we passed a team of women that had decided to practise digging snowholes instead.

Pressing on with heavy wet snow under our skis and big flakes smacking our faces, we began to feel that those sheltered snowholes were more and more attractive. With only another half-hour or so to the Jamtal, I succumbed to terminal boredom and announced, 'I'm not enjoying this; I'm going back.'

David immediately agreed but Jeff and Simon carried on, later claiming to have been most of the way up the Hinter Jamspitz, a good effort, though their knowledge of that depended entirely on a GPS altitude reading that they had taken in the murk.

After some messy skiing in poor visibility, David and I found the vacated snowholes just as the women were leaving, and we ducked in for a late lunch. With the pressure of the route lifted, David's mind turned to what had been troubling him back home. He opened up a bit, so I listened and made encouraging noises, but that's about all you can do in that situation.

Reunited at the hut, over the evening meal the team discussed personal best head-plants and whether our kick-turns had improved with all that practice, up and down. I had been able to watch David telemarking at his leisure, and there seemed little doubt that in deep soft snow with limited visibility, the slower telemark turn offered more stability.

In the cold air of the following morning, we set out carrying fully loaded rucksacks to our second base, the Silvretta Hut. On the climb up to the pass, Simon was having problems with his sled on the turns; the angles were just too acute. Now he knew how the dogs must have felt. Glorious sunshine greeted us at the Plan Rai Pass, so, stashing some of our loads in waterproof bivvi bags, we thought to take in the summit of Piz Fliana, 3281m.

It was possible to skin to within 100m of the west ridge, leaving little more than 200m to climb on foot, at first on steepening snow to the crest of the ridge, then along the mixed snow and rock of the ridge itself. But what must normally be a mixed scramble had become more serious under a blanket of deep snow. The point was emphasised when

Deep snow on Piz Fliana

I noticed that Simon, although a couple of metres from the snow edge, was actually climbing on the cornice itself with its break-line hidden under all the new snow. Rattled, David turned back at a steep step that was rendered particularly precarious by the unconsolidated snow covering the rocks needed for hand and foot holds. The rest of us struggled on through deepening snow, abandoning the difficult crest of the ridge to wade along its northern flank. Simon did sterling work breaking trail when I was left behind after making another attempt to force the ridge crest.

Just 30m below the summit we ran into another steep step that Simon wisely regarded as unjustifiable. I swam on a little, just to verify the bottomless snow, before agreeing and we turned back. Our track made the descent safer and quicker, but the attempt had taken us hours longer than expected, although the ski back down to the pass turned out to be the best snow of the tour.

Reunited with David, after lunch it was heads down for the slog up to the Silvrettapass. There had been lovely views, but cloud was building and by the time we gained the pass the weather had closed in,

High point on Piz Fliana

with dead flat light on the descent of the Silvretta Glacier to the hut. That didn't help my decidedly unstylish skiing, or our navigation through rolling hillocks of snow that provided no clues as to the whereabouts of the hut, until we stumbled upon it as the first big flakes of snow began falling. Somehow Simon still telemarked elegantly despite his loaded sled.

Inside, Urs, the guardian, talked to us about our intentions and seemed relieved that we were not planning to continue on the Silvretta Haute Route, but just intending to complete day tours before descending to Klosters; the weather forecast was in his opinion far too bad for anything more ambitious. Some guided parties had been worrying him with their determination to press on with the circuit. Later it was good to talk over that route for future reference, with the benefit of his hard-earned local knowledge recommending the best options for ski peaks on the way.

Next morning found us getting ready automatically, with thoughts of a modest excursion to the Rote Furka Pass, and the possibility of pressing on to the Schneeglocke if the weather cleared. When I stepped out through the hut door, skis and poles in hand, into driving snow and zero visibility, I had second thoughts; a good book seemed a better option. Life is too short! Simon, minus his sled, was keen to follow a guided party towards the Silvrettahorn, and Jeff and David agreed on the strength of a slight clearing in the weather.

I joined Walter Bonatti 'On the Heights', but within an hour Jeff and David were back. The guide had admitted that he'd been travelling in completely the opposite direction to the one he wanted. He'd corrected and pressed on, but his group did have a booking at the Wiesbadener Hut that evening. Simon had followed in his tracks, trusting to his GPS waypoints to get him back to our hut alone later. As the day wore on, with deteriorating weather and no sign of him, Urs grew increasingly anxious. A bearded bear of a man, he left Simon in no doubt about his feelings when, finally, Simon reappeared: 'You were alone. If something had happened to you, I would have had to go out to look for you, perhaps alone if your people did not want to go with me, and they had no obligation – but, as guardian, I did. And I have a newborn son in the valley!'

Later he mellowed, and since there was no one else in the hut that night, asked us what we would like for our evening meal as some options were possible. To lighten the mood I jokingly suggested pizza, something that I had never eaten in a hut. To my surprise, he took the suggestion seriously but explained that he couldn't make the dough base at such short notice. 'Perhaps tomorrow,' he offered and we jumped at the opportunity, although I wasn't sure that he wasn't planning some sort of practical joke.

That evening the tension in the day had made David more jumpy than he had been hitherto, although, to be fair, he had warned us at the outset of the trip that he had been suffering from a lot of stress at work. He was teaching at a time when schools were competing for shrinking numbers of students in an artificial marketplace in order to avoid the political unpopularity of planned school closures that had been created by previous Tory governments and continued by New Labour. League tables had put pressure on teachers, and self-management of schools had delivered extraordinary powers to headteachers. The more despotic had ruthlessly victimised teachers who they saw as any kind of threat to their authority or the marketing of the school. David seemed to have fallen foul of one of these characters, and had been off work for a time. This trip was part of his Cognitive Behavioural Therapy.

I knew all about that. I had watched people abandon honesty and integrity to further their personal interests, whether it be career advancement or enhanced pension, in the service of a narcissistic psychopath. The Thatcher period had encouraged an autocratic management model that turned too easily into a cult of leadership with fascist undertones that was diametrically opposed to what research had shown to be effective staff management. There were casualties; one way or another good people were damaged or destroyed. I knew one who had committed suicide. David was in danger of being one of them. He needed gentle handling.

In the morning, light snow was falling, but with the hidden sun lightening the sky above. We set out for the Schneeglocke, and the weather was no worse below the Rote Furka, so we continued. It's a steep pass which had big blocks of avalanche debris lying at its foot on this occasion, so Simon led the way, traversing in from further up the glacier, under the rocks of the Gletscherrücken to the east. Intimidated by the situation, David kept stopping and starting, forcing Jeff to do likewise. A heated exchange between them led to Jeff overtaking, putting in a new track, and I followed him. David colourfully conveyed his opinion of us and the route, with Jeff issuing curt dismissive responses before David stopped altogether, talking about turning back.

We all stopped. 'Leave it, Jeff,' I said. 'He's just wading through shit in his head; all the abuse, confrontations, arguments he's had at work coming to bear on this disagreement. Just ignore it and he'll calm down.'

Jeff grudgingly agreed, and Simon shuffled back to talk David into coming on up, but it was a tricky situation. I wouldn't have liked to see David going back to the hut on his own in the state he was in. Sometimes difficulties come from within as well as without. Regrouping, the pause had probably steadied us for the final steep kick-turns on the slope up to the broad col, but we kept the skins on to slide slowly down to a branch of the Klostertalergletscher beyond.

Urs had warned us about unstable snow slopes on the north side of the Gletscherrücken, so we kept left, skinning up snow-covered moraine ridges and glacier steps to reach a saddle at about 3100m. The wind was driving snow at us and my fingers were tingling into numbness, so we were lucky to find shelter for lunch in a windless snow bowl under a buttress of the Schneeglocke's final ridge. The hot tea made a big difference, and after lunch we skinned on up a snow slope until it was time to stash our skis and climb. Simon and Jeff went straight up untracked snow until they realised that we needed to traverse left to gain the ridge. The broad, wind-blasted ridge steepened towards the summit cross, where the weather relented to give us beautiful sunny views of a panorama of jagged snowy peaks.

Too cold to linger, we headed straight back down to the skis, bypassing our earlier false trails on new, heel-kicked steps. On ski, a fine descent in forgiving new snow found us under the Rote Furka again, and still able to follow the remains of our tracks to its blunt crest. Descending from the pass, Jeff nearly came to grief attempting kick-turns on the steep, difficult snow. It was painful to watch, so I shouted up that he should try hopping around with jump turns from a standing start and he fared better. There's something inherently unstable about kick-turns on really steep ground, the sort where you don't want to have each ski pointing in opposite directions when a gust of wind catches you off balance. On easier snow, more relaxed skiing took us

Simon experimenting with crossed haul-poles near the Silvretta Hut

back to the hut where a cheerful Urs announced that because of the weather no one else had arrived, so a celebratory pizza was on!

The final day broke with glowing distant summits. Later cloud still brought no snow, so the decision was reached to take Urs's advice and try for the Gletscherchamm, at 3173m, to the south of the Silvrettapass, before skiing the Verstanclagletscher down to Klosters. Taking our leave of Urs, despite our previous excursions, David set off enthusiastically in completely the wrong direction and the others failed to correct him despite my shouts from the rear, lost in the wind. Catching up, I finally got the message through but it was an up and down switchback across the glacier to get back on the right line. Storm clouds began to pile up quickly amongst the peaks, and it was snowing at the crossing of the Chremerchöpf, so we stopped to take stock while snacking. With no improvement likely there was no dissent about heading straight down in deteriorating weather. Despite cloud and snow flurries, the enclosing rock walls of the Verstanclagletscher were as spectacular as Urs had promised.

Forgiving snow beneath our skis compensated for the flat light, and we soon emerged below the worst of the weather. Poling nearly flat terrain led to a fast descent of narrow forest tracks, more poling down langlauf trails, and a welcome bus at Monbiel that finally delivered us to Klosters, where the sun shone for at least an hour before the rain came in.

The youth hostel was too full to accommodate us, but the staff allowed us to collect our kit and to shower; poling is a sweaty business, particularly after six days in the mountains, so they probably regarded that as a public duty. We were in Zurich that evening and in London within 24 hours.

We called it a draw with the weather, but in real terms the good days put us ahead. Coping with adversity is what adventures are all about, and we'd certainly had a varied mix of the unexpected and the difficult – but there was something satisfying about that, and the bonus for Simon was that he had thoroughly test-driven his new sled rig.

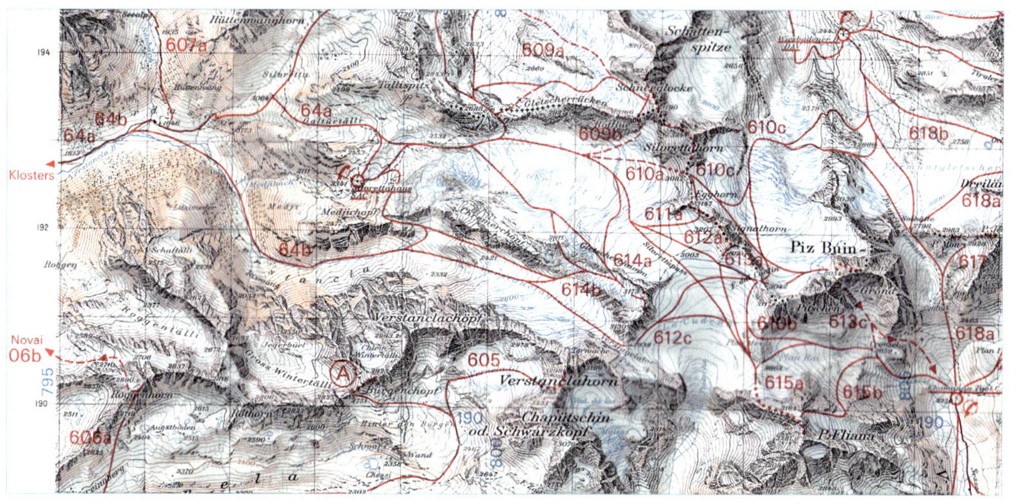

Silvretta map

6

AIGÜESTORTES – CARROS DE FOC

In 2001, my partner, Yvonne, had read an article about walking in the Parc Nacional d'Aigüestortes i Estany de Sant Maurici, to give it its full title, in the Pyrenees. Apparently, 'aigüestortes' means 'twisted waters' and refers to the multitude of streams linking many small lakes between the jagged peaks, all but a handful below 3000m. In October she could take a week's holiday, so a hut-to-hut trip was planned, walking and scrambling without having to worry too much about acclimatisation.

Our itinerary took us through a beautiful landscape with quality walking and scrambling routes, and it occurred to me that there might be ski-touring possibilities. I talked this over with Xavi, the guardian of Refugio d'Estany Llong, who told me, 'The huts usually open for February half-term holidays, when we can expect a lot of French customers, but if conditions are good, we'll stay open for as long as the season lasts' – he paused – 'providing we are getting the business. Some guardians get fed up and go back down to the comforts of the valley after days on their own with no customers turning up.'

The huts were either owned by different Catalan mountaineering associations or run privately, so whether they actually would be open was a bit hit-and-miss, but it was possible to phone around and vary the route if one or other of the huts was closed. A friend from Aragon recently commented that only in Catalunya could there be rival mountain associations. It's a joke, based on the feelings of many Spanish people that Catalan campaigns for independence have been threatening the hard-won constitution established after the Franco dictatorship. A full round of the huts is run as a race in the summer, named the Carros de Foc, Catalan for 'Chariots of Fire'.

Yvonne and I didn't manage the full circuit, but enough to whet my appetite for the winter; there were few opportunities to ski an extended hut-to-hut tour in February in the Alps. The lack of glaciers in the area would reduce the seriousness of the trip, but setting off so early in the season would suggest that the weather might be more extreme even this far south of the Alps.

Visitors from the UK were rare, and available information reflected that. Even when I tracked down route descriptions, they were in Catalan, which diverges from Spanish enough to cause some confusion in translation. I acquired a slim volume of selected ski tours including the Carros de Foc, and the appropriate Editorial Alpina maps. As with Italian maps, military control of cartography had led to some rather vague mapping, and variations on the names of features. The Pyrenees define the Spanish border with France, and in 1807 Napoleon had invaded Spain, installing his brother as its ruler. Too much detail in available maps might empower another enemy! There was an exploratory sense about this adventure from the start.

I assembled a team of Alpine Club members that I'd known for some time, and planned the trip for the week after the French half-term to avoid the crowds. Denis had skied the Haute Route with me, Mike Pinney and Jeff Harris had climbed with me in the Alps, and Mike Parsons was a mutual friend and experienced ski-mountaineer who had been the managing director of Karrimor before semi-retirement. It was Mike Pinney's first hut-to-hut tour, and Denis had suffered a serious accident from which he was making an incredible recovery, so there was no macho bullshit about us; just a bunch of mates out to explore an area little known to British skiers or climbers.

We drove from Barcelona via Lleida, passing crags glinting with bolt lines, to reach Espot, where a woman in the tourist office was full of information about the huts and made all the bookings, as well as selling maps to the mapless in the team. Refugios J.M. Blanc and Colomina were unwardened, so she worked out a route with us that bypassed those two huts. Spending the night at a local *hostal,* I ended up in a stuffy smokers' room, and I later found there was no bracket to hold the shower-head and control the powerful water pressure; taking a shower was like wrestling with a snake, but I survived.

In the morning, we drove up to Super-Espot, the little ski resort above Espot, where Mike Pinney and I were offered bargain ski passes by a girl whose two friends had let her down. Shortly afterwards a Guardia Civil skier bore down on us and I thought we were going to be charged for breaking some by-law on ski passes, but he only wanted to warn us about a storm coming in that afternoon; a kindness we were to find replicated amongst the people of this mountain community. He'd seen the rucksacks and touring bindings, so supposed that we would be heading off from the top of the lift system to ski down to Refugio J.M. Blanc. It's normally a good start to the trip but, with the hut closed, not an option for us this time.

After skiing a few runs Jeff and I decided to make a reconnaissance by skinning up the road from the highest ski lift while the rest of the team continued to regain their 'ski legs' on piste. The snowed-up road petered out a few score metres from Point 2657m, the northernmost summit of a ridge that culminates in Pic de Sudorn 2708m. Topping out in a grey wind carrying flakes of snow, we looked down on an apparently amenable ski run to Refugio J.M. Blanc on the shores of Estany Tort, but snow was thinly distributed and that seemed likely to be the case on the traverse to Refugio Colomina, which probably explained the closure of these southernmost huts. The previous autumn, J.M. Blanc had not been staffed, but Yvonne and I had been equipped for an unstaffed hut and made the traverse from J.M. Blanc to Estany Llong in 6–7 hours when the Colomina Hut had been locked; I remember the prayer flags fluttering from the Refugio's porch as we passed.

Jeff and I turned back, finding technical skiing down the Pala d'Eixe, avoiding snow-scattered scree interspersed with patches of barely covered winter grass, the longer stalks waving above a snow-matted tangle, and slaloming around the avalanche barriers that were holding nothing back. That obstacle course delivered us into a snow bowl leading easily to the piste. After a few more runs, it was time to return to Espot and make use of the licensed taxi service, the only way to drive up the road to Sant Maurici, before they stopped running for the day. At the

Refugio Estany Llong

lakeside of Estany Sant Maurici, the weather had closed in, with gusts swirling spindrift into the falling snow, but the way up to the hut was short and sheltered through the pines, just ten minutes from the road. A long low building with small shuttered windows and a massive stone chimney on one wall, Refugio Ernest Mallefré was half-hidden by drifts piled against the walls, suggesting that the door might need digging out in a season of heavy snowfall. The female guardian gave us a cheerful welcome, recognising me from my previous visit.

The storm should have cleared by morning, but showed little sign of letting up and put down a metre of snow in the course of the day. Denis discovered that he had left his waterproof overtrousers at the *hostal* in Espot, so he and Mike Parsons made good use of the enforced rest day by skiing down the road to collect them. The rest of us read and talked, huddled around the excellent stove with its crackling logs and scent of woodsmoke, while the guardian shovelled snow in an attempt to keep the approach to the hut clear. Later she cooked up tortilla for lunch.

A lone French snow-shoer arrived with his husky, and later another huge dog turned up on his own, probably having attached himself to a French team of seven who had arrived not long before him. When our MD returned with Denis, he chatted fluently with the French group, the rest of us occasionally included in the conversation when they deigned to speak a little English. Both dogs slept outside, curled up in the snow, although the big one made some serious attempts to muscle in through the doorway at any opportunity. The guardian had kindly phoned ahead to rearrange our onward hut bookings.

The next morning saw us taking turns to break trail through deep snow along the forestry road heading for Portarró d'Espot. The French team followed, taking advantage of our efforts and then, about halfway there, moved into the lead and took turns with trail-breaking. The huge dog was still following them despite efforts to discourage him. There was plenty of sunshine and wind, but hazy clouds hid the peaks at times, hinting at the possibility of snow.

Stopping for lunch on the Portarró Pass, the dog begged shamelessly from all of us but must have preferred the French offerings since he followed them up into the cloud still hanging about Pic del Portarró. My team decided to pass on the pic in favour of a good ski down while the visibility lasted. This proved to be a wise move, particularly with tricky snow and an uncertain line through the trees. Eventually this became a plod along the frozen shallows of Estany Llong, wondering about the thickness of the ice under our skis. At the outflow of the lake, we climbed up to the summer road, which quickly took us to the hut. There had been more sunny spells but the peaks remained mostly lost in cloud.

Refugio Estany Llong was bigger than Mallefré, but stone-built in the same traditional style. Despite the sunshine, inside the hut the open fire struggled to deal with the cold as we crouched over it trying to dry our inner boots and gloves. Meanwhile the pair of guardians worked in the kitchen or took occasional breaks to add to their tally of pull-ups, meticulously recorded on a clipboard at the bar. Xavi, one of the authors of a Pyrenean Hot Rock guidebook to the area, gave us the benefit of his advice on the next leg of our journey over the Coll de Contraix. He too recognised me and remembered our conversation about ski-touring possibilities. Later that afternoon the radiators came on, and the place warmed up for the evening meal.

Wind had gusted outside the attic dormitory most of the night and a morning that had been forecast to be fine dawned blowy and snowy. This wasn't inspiring, but the team consensus was that it was clear enough to 'have a go'. As we left, Xavi was concerned enough to come over: 'You don't have to go up, you know.' I waited expectantly. 'You can ski down to Boi and take a taxi up to the dam at Cavallers, reaching the Refugio Ventosa y Cavell more easily from there. This is an army day.'

I looked at him blankly, 'An army day? What do you mean?'

'Only the army goes out on days like this.'

… not a bunch of wimpy Brits on tour, I mentally completed for him, but actually said, 'Well, we'll see how it goes, and can always retreat and do that if it's too bad up there.' It was good to have a contingency plan.

A fast ski down the snowy road, before turning off to take precarious skinning tracks on snow packed on the wood of narrow footbridges across the main river and one of its tributaries, led us out of the trees and onto a thinly snow-covered track waymarked with painted stumps and cairns. The weather continued intimidating with snow squalls that never quite closed in enough to turn us back.

At the head of the valley, in an impressive cirque, a lone chamois plunged off through the snow drifts. A stiff climb to the right and a little higher than absolutely necessary, acting on Xavi's advice to avoid avalanche danger, left us with a slightly descending traverse to Estany de Contraix, the little lake frozen solid. There the wind rapidly chilled us while we waited for our MD to repair a faulty skin, before clambering over boulders and skinning along the margins of the lake ice to reach the final slopes.

The last 30m or so to the Coll de Contraix were blown clear of snow, and were in any case too steep to climb on ski, but we found shelter beneath a rock buttress below the crest of the pass to strip skins and strap skis to our packs for the climb. It wasn't easy to step into the icy blast on the crest, but we stumbled down frozen gravel on the other side to reach the snow and were soon back on ski.

Visibility chose to deteriorate just then, and some desperate survival skiing down steep slopes followed. No matter how defensively we skied, all of us found ourselves suddenly airborne at one time or another as

Final climb to gain Collet de Contraix

the snow beneath our skis dropped away from an unseen step. Some of us fell further than others. Some retained their skis, some didn't, but luckily none of us lost a ski.

The angle eased and visibility improved as we passed vague lakelets of flat ice and threaded our way through boulder slopes. Just as I spotted traces of old ski tracks leading up to the hut above Estany Negre, Jeff managed to end up knee-deep in water, as new snow had masked the thinness of the lake ice beneath it. He squelched out and we stepped up to the Refugio Ventosa y Cavell, where the guardian and her partner were surprised to see this bunch of dishevelled Brits appearing out of the storm.

She phoned Xavi to let him know of our arrival, so they must have expected us to turn back. Much interest in conditions on the route was expressed in the warmth of the big modern hut where the dining room housed a large stove although the dorm and washroom were both freezing – steam rose from an arcing stream of golden piss when I had finally rehydrated enough to want to go.

The forecast good weather in the morning didn't arrive as wind and snowfall continued. An update to the forecast suggested improvement by lunchtime, but the peaks were hidden in a cloud canopy all day. A brightening in the afternoon tempted the others out to skin up to one of lakes above the hut, just to recce the route, but I stayed in to dig Jack Kerouac, 'On the Road' with Dean Moriarty and the other beats. Not at all the same road travelled as ours.

The early evening was spent repairing the hinge on our MD's right boot. Scrounging a bolt and improvising washers from the warden's bits and pieces, Mike's skills as a helicopter designer were attended by a rapt audience; there wasn't a lot else to do. When our excellent dinner arrived, the conversation turned to vegetarianism. Mike commented in sombre tones that his girlfriend, Susannah, '… is one when it suits her.' Jeff grimly nodded his assent as the wind rattled the shutters, and it all sounded very sinister.

'Did she eat someone's pet hamster when they weren't looking?' I asked innocently.

Next day dawned clear and crisp, although streams of high cirrus floated through the blue of the sky as our harscheisen bit into icy crust at 8 am. At first the sun didn't reach us, passing Estany de Traverssani, but as it gained height the shadows of the surrounding mountains shrank and patches of strange rich light caught us, as if on a stage set, as we passed through them, casting our own long shadows on the glittering snow.

Reaching Estany de Mangades, we climbed up to a slight saddle in the low ridge separating that lake from Estany de les Monges, then skinned straight across the frozen surface of the upper lake, confident that the ice would support our weight at this altitude. Traversing below Port d'Onhla Crestada, we overtook groups that had come over that pass from the Restanca Hut on our ascent to the east ridge of Montardo.

We traversed below a big rock buttress on the ridge to find a hidden col just to the right of it, which Jeff crossed to put in a good track up the other side of the ridge to reach another col, where I decided to leave my rucksack. Ahead, the steep summit slopes were criss-crossed by yesterday's tracks, and one by one each of us began picking our own lines up them, trying not to be caught out by awkward kick-turns on the acute angles of each zig and zag where churned snow could initiate a slide. Jeff slowed and began to regret taking his rucksack, which raised his centre of gravity.

A guide and his client were coming up fast on us, so I took a line on the flank of the slope and ridge above, breaking trail between rocks through firmer snow (but not racing of course!) and just managing to beat them to the first ascent of the day. The guide's disappointment was written all over his face when he popped up on the crest of the ridge behind me.

At 2,833m the views were incredibly clear; east to Andorra and Pica d'Estats, and west to the Aneto-Maladeta massif and along the chain of the Pyrenees to Vignemale and Néouvielle. The summit became crowded with French teams amidst much excitement, and then the rest of my team arrived. I zipped all zips against the cold, stripped off skins, took pictures and posed for others, never quite seriously. A guide with three clients led the first team off, tipping over a distinct edge, and I followed, relishing the steepness of the slope, skiing back to my rucksack on the col. This offered a good place to regroup for the next stage of the descent, so I waited, watching gripped skiers going for the turns, missing them, tumbling, sliding. Luckily the slope was short, with a safe runout where it eased; no one was likely to slide over a precipice.

Mike found the skiing challenging but our MD kept close and gave advice that helped. It was remarkable how he had taken our novice ski-tourer under his wing, and Mike certainly appreciated it. Once the rest of the team had collected and sorted their sacks, we headed back along the east ridge and over the hidden col.

Instead of following tracks back towards Port d'Onhla Crestada, we continued traversing east around the head of the cirque, crossing high up the spur that descended to divide Estany de les Monges from Estany de Mangades, then skiing lovely snow steeply down to the lake shore south of Estany del Port de Caldes. Over lunch, our MD and Denis told us of the eagle that had soared past them as they skied the ridge. After the break, a 150m climb on untracked snow took us to the Port de Caldes, with fine views back towards Montardo.

Another eagle, or perhaps the same one, circled overhead before slipping beyond a ridge while we stripped skins before skiing beyond

Montardo from Port de Caldes

the Port. Open snow slopes were fun but slaloming around large humps and bumps prompted our MD and Denis to check navigation. Peering uncertainly at their maps one asked, 'Have you got your reading glasses?'

'No,' replied the other, 'I haven't got them out. What about you?'

'Left them in Espot, I'm afraid.'

'Oh.'

They continued to study maps that they couldn't read for some minutes before giving up. Looking over Denis's shoulder, I worked out that we had to descend the gorge-like El Garganta valley below, which led directly to the Colomèrs Hut. While Denis and his partner in navigation investigated some unlikely untracked bumps, the rest of us shot off to the hut, a modern construction perched on a domed granite outcrop above a dam that enhanced the capacity of the Lac Major de Colomèrs.

When our MD arrived, it was to reveal that the hinge on his left boot had now broken so Mike was involved in more repairs before the evening meal was provided by a surly guardian. The MD still had a

Skiing from Port de Caldes

professional interest in new technology, but sometimes its very newness let him down. Field-testing new outdoor gear never seems to be very rigorous, and there have even been recalls on essential safety gear like bindings or transceivers.

The guardian's dog seemed as miserable as the guardian. Perhaps it was living with the outside loo, a traditional long-drop affair with a remarkable paper blowback effect if the wind was in the wrong direction. I suppose what else might be blown back would depend on the strength of the wind. That wouldn't account for the dog, though; perhaps misery really does like company.

The night had been clear at 10 pm but leaden skies greeted us in the morning and the guardian announced that there was no hot water for our flasks, which was a blow and wouldn't have needed a lot of effort for him to organise. He also took no interest in us or our route, so would have been unable to answer any queries if we hadn't turned up at the Amitges Hut. This was the one unfriendly character that we met on the tour.

Skinning towards the second Col Port de Ratera de Colomèrs

We could have crossed the Còth deth Tuc Gran de Sendrosa, taking in the summit of the Tuc Gran de Sendrosa and spending the night at the Saboredo Hut, but it was closed. Instead, we slid down below the dam then skinned up between two rock buttresses to cross a low ridge and continue up the valley beyond. The head of the valley steepened to a double pass; on the near side the Port de Ratera de Colomèrs, wind-licked with spindrift, with the Tuc de Ratera, looking rugged and difficult, looming to the right, and the further Port de Ratera d'Espot, which could also be reached from the Refugio de Saboredo.

The route onto the Tuc de Ratera wasn't obvious, and there was sufficient disagreement for three separate routes to be tried. Mike and Jeff, armed with axes and crampons, set off up a couloir and onto rock. Denis and the MD traversed to the south and climbed mostly snow from the far side. I followed cairns and old ski tracks on what I took to be the 'ordinary route', but it was steep, and the tracks soon disappeared. All of us gained the summit within a few minutes of each other but, unable to evaluate the relative merits of each of our individual

routes, loyally followed them back down. As experienced mountaineers, we tended to know our own minds about routes and then stick to them, perhaps a little too possessively at times.

Denis and the MD skied directly into the valley beyond and, after I had rejoined Jeff and Mike, the three of us descended from the col. It wasn't long before we all realised that the valley wasn't the key to reaching the Amitges Hut, as we'd have to climb the ridge bounding it to the east, where tracks came over a little col. The scrappy ski down from that col was disappointing but the stunning scenery, approaching the hut from the north, compensated for that as we skinned across the flat ice of Estany Gran d'Amitges dominated by the granite towers of the Agulla d'Amitges.

The Refugio d'Amitges had the best facilities of the tour, with hot showers – a luxury after so many unwashed days. Drying kit with the stove burning and snow banked under a picture window outside, we

Above: Crossing Estany Gran d'Amitges
Right: Descending Tuc de Saboredo

could see white ridges and peaks glimmering ghostly in the hazy moonlight.

On the last day of the tour, light sacks were packed for a morning raid on the Tuc de Saboredo, skinning past the Agulla d'Amitges to reach a saddle behind the towers. From there, snow slopes led up to the south ridge of the Tuc. Soon it was too steep for skis, and as we climbed towards the ridge the snow became steeper and deeper with more floundering than step-kicking. We reached a high point on the ridge to see the true summit beyond a narrow, dangerously corniced, section. With snow sliding away beneath our feet, this was as far as we were safely going to get.

Quickly reversing the route, we realised that there was still time for another try from the Coll d'Amitges, on the north ridge, traversing on ski to a point below it then skinning up. With a more northerly aspect, the snow conditions were better, and this time we made it to the summit. Better still, there was perfect corn snow all the way back to the hut.

Repacking rucksacks at the Refugio, all that remained for us was to ski down the icy road to Estany St Maurici and take a taxi back to Espot. A mid-winter visit to this enclave in the Pyrenees had been challenging but well worth the effort – and, for me, had begun a relationship with those mountains that continues to this day.

***

Wikiloc | Ruta CARROS DE FOC, COMPLETO (see Maps & QR Codes p.229) offers computerised maps which you can zoom in on to follow the route. Mapas ráster and the OpenTopoMap I found the easiest to use.

7

WAPTA ICEFIELDS TRAVERSES

Using staffed huts as bases or linking them in longer tours allows ski-mountaineers to venture into mountain areas that become more remote in winter when any forestry roads or walking trails are blocked by snow. Instead, when you are on ski, it is glaciers that become the main thoroughfares of the mountains, linked by passes at their heads from which it may be possible to climb the mountains that surround those glaciers. Self-sufficiency is required in travelling in such areas, but not necessarily in the huts themselves, particularly in the Alps. Cooked meals are available in heated dining rooms and blankets in dormitories, all supplied from the valley by helicopter in most cases, and co-ordinated by the guardian.

However, there are more remote areas where the number of visitors is too low to justify building large huts or basing a member of staff in them, and national parks where helicopter flights are strictly regulated. Canada is the second largest country in the world, yet has a population about the same as the UK – concentrated, as always, in the cities. There's a lot of wilderness. In 1936, Georg von Lillienfeld noted in the *Canadian Alpine Journal,*

The characteristic difference that strikes the European visitor almost on his first day in the Canadian Rockies and impresses itself more and more profoundly upon his mind during a longer stay, may be seen correctly in the tremendous vastness and still unspoiled wilderness of these rugged ranges and trailless valleys and the complete solitude of the 'high country' and the big icefields. Although detailed maps with ski routes, major crevasses and avalanche gullies marked on them, an elaborately set up hut system, human settlements in every little valley have done a great deal to lessen the dangers of skiing and ski-mountaineering in the Alps, they have also taken away a good part of the fun that lies for the experienced mountaineer in being dependent only on his own ability in pioneering excursions off the beaten path. ('A Spring Excursion into the Bow Lake District,' CAJ 24.)

In those areas the ski-mountaineer must bring all that he or she needs to such huts as exist. Pioneers built huts, but not many, and most were only useful for summer mountaineering. An exception is the Wapta Icefields area between Lake Louise and Jasper, both centres for mountain tourism, winter and summer. There the mountains are very suitable for ski mountaineering, and some huts are accessible from the road in a day. Glaciers will still demand crevasse-rescue equipment, and low temperatures will mean that sufficient warm clothing is needed, but for unstaffed huts a sleeping bag and all food to be consumed, perhaps even a stove, fuel and cooking pot, will also have to go into the rucksack. It's a significant additional load with which to climb and ski, increasing the commitment of the adventure, although granting access to mountains where it's possible to be the only team on the summit, or route, in country that belongs as much, if not more, to the wolf and the bear as to you.

2006

In 2006, I had already become involved in expedition skiing but that was all new to my partner, Adele. Her son, Adam, was working as a chef for the season in Sunshine, the ski resort just outside Banff. He too was interested in our plans. He'd learnt to ski but later converted to snowboarding. Now he wanted to try the adventure of ski-touring. Adele arranged for us to spend the last week of March at Sunshine, luxuriating in hot tubs after days on and off piste, with the occasional warm-up tour. I booked some nights at Alpine Club of Canada backcountry huts in the Wapta Icefields to follow.

There was actually some sunshine at Sunshine and we skied gated off-piste runs like Delirium Dive, which didn't open to allow you access until the gate registered your transceiver signal. Skinning up onto Twin Cairns was also an easy warm-up day tour. I managed to break a ski by some over-enthusiastic mogul-skiing, and had to go into Banff to replace the pair. To my disgust, the shop would not fit the bindings I was using at the time onto a new pair of skis. 'Too old!' they told me, so I had to shell out for new bindings as well, although I made sure that I kept the old ones. It was my first pair of 'fat' skis with pin bindings. Luckily, I still had a couple of days of piste-skiing to get used to them.

The resort was closing down when we skied out, but Adam would be involved with all that for a further week, so Adele and I decamped to Lake Louise and arranged transport to drop us on the approach to the Stanley Mitchell Hut next day.

Our taxi picked us up from the youth hostel early, driving up the Icefields Parkway towards Jasper, but turning off for Field, thereby crossing the Great Divide over the Kicking Horse Pass, which finally linked British Columbia by rail to the rest of Canada in the 19th century. We were dropped off at the parking lot by the turn-off to Cathedral Mountain Chalets as the road into the valley in that direction was closed by a locked gate and left unploughed. It was 23 km to the Stanley Mitchell Hut, but the guidebook described an enclosed camp shelter with firewood at the Takakkaw Falls campground, about halfway. If we found the journey was taking too much out of us, it seemed we could stop there overnight. The use of names drawn from the languages of indigenous peoples was a reminder that those peoples had lived in harmony with the land of North America for perhaps 13,000 years, according to the latest archaeology.

During the 5 km climb up switchbacks on the snow-covered road to the campground, we were haunted by mournful hootings of locomotives winding their slow way invisibly through the spiral tunnels carved out of the mountain to reduce the incline for the trains of freight cars that seemed to stretch for a kilometre or more. The deserted road's hairpins seemed to be functioning in a similar way to the spiral tunnels, but with a lot more human effort.

Curtains of ice fringed with icicles hung from seepage along slanting bedding planes in the buttresses around us that rose to rugged summits. Beyond the switchbacks the road went straight on to the campground, but was threatened by avalanches from Wapta mountain; big open chutes between shallow ridges with wide shelves of cornices up on the summit ridge, but no signs of fresh avalanche debris. We hurried through as fast as possible.

At the campground the grubby shelter was not very well enclosed, with broken windows and what wood there was too damp and chunky to make a fire easily. We decided to push on to the hut that day. Takakkaw Falls leapt in a streak of ice straight down the cliff above the campground.

So far, we had more or less followed the course of the Yoho River, but beyond the campground the trail entered thickening forest. The guidebook acknowledged that this section of the route passing Laughing Falls can be hard to follow in the trees, and that was confirmed by the fact that we never saw anything like a frozen waterfall. The river flowed, a thread of open water, between banks of snow. Fortunately, there were tracks to follow from a previous party, which must have set off ahead of us.

Those tracks enabled us to locate the turn-off left taking the valley of the Little Yoho River, the trail zigzagging up through ancient forest before easing and slanting back towards the river. Keeping to the north bank, we continued traversing into the valley as it levelled with open glades appearing amongst the trees. The hut itself was located in trees on the north side of one of these glades, but could easily have been missed in bad weather with poor visibility.

It had taken us nine and a half hours of skinning to get to the hut, and whilst my feet were fine Adele's were badly blistered. It felt so good to finally have respite, reaching the historic hut, shared on this occasion with only a handful of other skiers. A small guided party was planning to cross the Wapta Icefield to the north-east to reach the Bow Hut, hopefully in a day but they were carrying bivouac equipment just in case. Brynne and Frank were planning to ski routes around the hut for a few days, as we were. That night, after everyone had settled into

Arriving at the Stanley Mitchell Hut

the attic dormitory, leaving the hatch to the stairs open to benefit from the rising heat of the stove, we found we were sharing the hut with something else.

There was a shout; 'Something ran across my face!'

The guide shot bolt upright in his sleeping bag, flashing his torch around. There was a blur of movement, a scrabble of claws and it was gone back down the hatch.

'What the hell was that?' One of the clients asked.

'Pine marten, I think,' the guide replied. 'I reckon we should close the hatch. If you react when it runs over you, they can give you a nasty bite.'

He slammed the hatch down and shot the bolt.

We all settled down, but not for long. The pine marten began to scrabble at the hatch coupled with a kind of shrieking. The people bedded nearest banged the hatch in return and after a few exchanges, the animal gave up, though there were other sounds from the room below.

In the morning, it was clear that the hatch had been splintered in places where teeth and claws had ripped at the wood, and the kitchen

Pine marten in the woodpile

had been raided. There was more mess than loss, largely because a lot of stuff was wrapped, or in containers concealing its scent. Pemmican and jerky were the main casualties, but the raid created a sense of insecurity. To lose food was serious; 'There sure as hell ain't any shops up here!' as Frank put it.

There was some puzzlement about how the pine marten had got in. Historically, the first huts in the icefields had been trashed by wolverines, which led to up-grading their construction, but here the doors and windows were locked and sound, whilst there was no sign of damage from a forced entry. The animal was very territorial, which seemed to indicate it had been there for a while.

I spent the early morning chopping wood while Adele allowed her blisters time to dry out and do some healing. Afterwards, sitting quietly reading, I noticed a pair of bright eyes staring out of the woodpile in the hut. Keeping perfectly still, I watched as the pine marten ran across to the fireplace, climbed easily up the stone surround and slipped between the steel blanking plate that closed off the chimney and the stone. Closing the fireplace meant the stove-pipe went through the centre of the blanking plate, and the chimney should otherwise have been sealed, but some of the sealant must have deteriorated or been scratched away.

Later Adele felt she could manage to skin up to Kiwetinok Pass for an easy half-day, getting our bearings in some inspiring scenery. The weather began to deteriorate as the afternoon went on, but we climbed beyond Kiwetinok Lake to the pass itself and only later, during the descent, lost definition in flat light.

The pine marten had been keeping a low profile with all the people around the hut in the evening, but there was a group decision to keep the door to the kitchen locked that night to avoid any more depredations of our food supplies. When we went to bed, the hatch went down and we felt a lot safer than before. Not for long. An enraged beast first attacked the hatch to the dorm, then appeared to be doing the same downstairs to the kitchen door. Eventually, armed with headtorch, ski pole and ice axe, I went down after it. The animal had torn away wood on the kitchen door and more from the attic hatch, so I chased it around the main room, brandishing the ice axe defensively and hoping it would think twice about its occupation of the hut. The creature obviously knew its territory and took refuge behind bench seats backed against the walls of the room. I managed to pull some forward to maintain pursuit but it leapt up at me, teeth bared, before beating a retreat up the chimney. There was peace for a while, but later more scratching at the kitchen door could be heard. At least it was no longer drawing attention to itself by screeching.

In the morning, Adele's blisters were still troubling her and she didn't feel up to much, but over breakfast Brynne and Frank asked if I wanted to go out with them. They were from Portland, Oregon, but had little experience on glaciers and wanted to try the route to President Pass. They had all the crevasse-rescue gear, but not much idea of how to use it. Adele seemed fine with the plan, and I gave the couple a quick run-through of crevasse-rescue techniques, reminding them that if nothing else, they would have to hold the victim while he or she prussiked out of the crevasse. A party of three would definitely be safer. I also suggested going to Emerald Pass, similar in height gain and angle, but with a smaller area of glaciated terrain to pass through.

Setting off for Emerald Pass, the route onto President Pass opened up to our left, looking very beautiful under a slightly hazy blue sky. The

Brynne and Frank deciding to go for the President Pass, in the background

slanting strata of the long north-west ridge of the President held bands of snow, reminding me of a tilted layer cake, and the glacier looked benign. I was tempted. It had been their first choice so I could tell Frank and Brynne were tempted too. We swung left and began the long climb.

I broke trail all the way, aiming to avoid any hint of crevasses, pausing at times to make sure that Brynne and Frank were both okay with what we were doing. Looking back, I could see the forest rising above the hut to treeless slopes below Isolate Peak and Isolate Col, which led into the traverse north and east to the Bow Hut. Mt McArthur rose to the north-west, offering another fine ski-mountaineering objective.

Roped up and gaining height, we could see over the north ridge of the Vice President to Mt Balfour, the Waputik Icefield and the site of the Scott Duncan Hut, which Adele and I were hoping to visit in the next phase of our trip. By the time we reached the pass, the sky had filled with thin cloud, filtering the sunshine. There was no way we could climb the steep, stepped ridges of either peak on ski and too much deep snow to consider it on foot but the pass was a wild place.

I looked far down to where the frozen surface of Emerald Lake lay amidst forest to the south, while nearby a cornice like a great balcony of snow projected north from the point where the east ridge of the President steepened above the pass.

Stripping skins, we skied back down the line of the descent, making little excursions into more interesting terrain at times, and throughout enjoying fantastic powder. Cloud had become denser, greying the blue of the sky, and in the latter stages of the descent, flat light meant more cautious skiing.

Back at the hut, Adele reported no further sightings of the pine marten, but her blisters still looked angry and I could understand her wish not to exacerbate the inflammation by going out next day after Frank and Brynne had left. Instead, we practised ropework and crevasse-rescue techniques. I'd forgotten it was my birthday, but Adele had not; she'd brought up a mini champagne bottle and some fine Swiss chocolate to celebrate. 'What a star!' I noted in my journal. Again, there was no trouble from the pine marten that night, but who could tell what would meet the next visitors to the hut?

Our time was up next morning, so we packed to ski out down the Little Yoho Valley. There was some crazy fun following the winding icy track through the trees, especially when it steepened, with crusted heavy snow off-track bringing us to an abrupt halt when we hit it; a kind of emergency brake, if needed, although with the probability it would result in a tumble. At Takakkaw Falls we met a couple looking remarkably fresh who confessed to having hired a skidoo to bring them in that far. That was strictly against the National Park rules, but I have to admit that after 11 km of wearying slush finally put us back at the pick-up point for our taxi Adele and I were sorry to have missed it. I was sure some of those switchbacks climbed rather than descended as we skated and free-heeled around them.

Taking a day off in Lake Louise while we waited for Adam to join us, I found myself suffering from a nasty cold and dosed up on paracetamol. Adam's mate Sven had asked if he could join us, since he'd heard a lot about the traverse of the Wapta Icefields from others in the ski patrol, but had never had an offer to get it done. Sven was a New Zealander of Swiss-German extraction who worked the ski-fields of New Zealand in the austral winter and at Sunshine in the Canadian winter. He told me he had done some previous touring and seemed to know what he was talking about, so I had no objections to taking him along. Sven made his hut bookings by phone that day.

Early next morning, Adele and I met the lads and took Adam off to be kitted out with rental gear before being dropped at 9.30 am at a small parking lot a couple of kilometres beyond Bow Summit on the Icefields Parkway.

Initially skiing along a snowed-up forest road, once we turned off into the trees Adam had one of the worst possible reintroductions to skiing; an icy ski track winding and rolling down to the shore of Peyto Lake. Where the track wasn't polished ice, it was collapsing snow, a daunting combination, but he survived. With skins on, the lake was a much easier matter, well frozen and covered with a good layer of snow. There were tracks to follow but the delta at the head of the lake seemed a long way off. We skinned on cheerfully, getting used to the roar of avalanches pouring off the sunny flanks of Caldron Peak above.

Snow was thinner on the pebbly outwash of the delta, with sparse brushwood standing clear above it, as the shady north face of Mt Jimmy Simpson towered above us to the south. Peyto Creek appeared briefly where the trail began to rise through more or less snow-covered moraine banks in the narrowing valley, but bad snow slipped away treacherously and my cold was giving me a hard time by then. Steep awkward moraine meant some tough skinning with one or other of us deciding at times to carry skis and climb on foot.

The building in the distance was taken to be the hut by the lads, and although I knew otherwise, I let the illusion encourage them to persevere in the tricky conditions. Reaching the glaciology research station, I had to tell them that the hut lay a further 2 km beyond, but by then most of the difficulties were over. We roped up for the glacier, only to be passed by two guys skinning along side by side, who seemed completely unconcerned about crevasse danger. Arriving at the Peyto Hut at 5 pm, we felt it had been a long day.

There were several teams at the hut, either planning to make day tours or to take off on the traverse. My plan was to do both; traverse from hut to hut but climb a peak at each, weather permitting. The next day was scheduled for us to climb Mt Rhondda, so I asked around about conditions as we sorted out our evening meal.

Adam, Adele and Sven after crossing Peyto Lake

A team of five Canadians had been up there that day and were happy to advise: 'The route goes almost due south to climb back north, up the end of the south-east ridge of Rhondda, avoiding crevasses on its north-east face. We didn't go that far though, just climbed more steeply up a spur about half way along the ridge.'

I asked the obvious question: 'What about crevasses?'

'Oh, there's been loads of snow this season that's pretty much filled them up. There's been no snowfall since, so just follow our tracks and you'll be fine.'

We shared a table with two women, and one of them asked me, 'Are you British?'

'Yeah, although I know my accent isn't the most widely known. Adele and Adam are also Brits, and Sven is a New Zealander.' I completed the introductions.

Bernice was from the Netherlands and lived in Fernie for the skiing, travelling for assignments with *National Geographic*. She introduced her friend, and asked, 'Do you know Joe Simpson?'

'Not really. I mean I've met him at various Alpine Club and Climbers' Club events, the Kendal Mountain Festival, and we have mutual friends like Terry Gifford who runs the Mountain Literature Festival at Bretton Hall. I'd strike up a conversation with him but I doubt that he'd remember me. I've read his stuff, of course.'

'I just wondered,' Bernice continued. 'I spent time with Yossi Brain in La Paz; you have a similar accent, I think. Joe climbed with him, but Joe seemed to be so accident-prone, even with little things about the house. I wondered if you'd noticed.'

'Well, all I know is from the books, and he's certainly had his share of accidents. Speaking of accidents, what do you think of the crevasse danger on the icefields?'

'Not much, I think. We came over from the Bow Hut without roping up.'

'Perhaps we should have done?' her friend suggested, but Bernice was dismissive.

When there's local advice, it's worth listening to, so next morning I told the team to follow exactly in my tracks, and the rope was carried by Sven as last man.

The Canadian team had left obvious tracks across the Peyto Glacier, then heading up a vague spur on the north-east flank of Mt Rhondda, although a cold wind had sprung up, blowing spindrift which was beginning to obscure them. Adele was sensibly pacing herself to avoid more blister damage, so I pressed on to be sure where the tracks reached the spur, leaving my fresh tracks for the others to follow.

Once onto the main ridge I could wait in safety, and it was just as I thought I'd reached that point when there was a muffled boom and the snow dropped away below my skis. Realising instantly what had happened, I braced myself for impact on the ice of the crevasse below, but instead found my fall broken in a depth of soft snow. *Great! Now all I have to do is climb out,* went through my head. Then the roof fell in. The rest of the snow bridge for some metres around the hole I'd made fell in on top of me, burying me completely.

I remember being very annoyed – *I was exactly on the Canadian team's tracks!* Then turned to the practical issues about getting myself out. And found that I couldn't. I'd thrashed around as much as possible to create an air pocket after the burial but despite that the sheer weight of snow was pinning me down. No matter how I fought, I could not free my legs – still attached to skis I guessed – or my left arm, pinned by heavy snow blocks. There were some moments of panicky cursing as I struggled uselessly to free myself, but this wasn't an avalanche burial. I could breathe, and my right arm was free to clear snow away from my face and open up a kind of snow tunnel to where light filtered through suggesting that I wasn't buried too deeply. The helplessness was very difficult to deal with but I suppressed my feelings. There was no way I was going to get out on my own and therefore nothing to do but wait for the rest of my team to arrive.

The time taken before I heard voices couldn't have been as long as it felt, stuck there with no hope of self-rescue. I was glad that I hadn't removed too much clothing on the ascent, and my rucksack was keeping my back warm. Eventually I thought I heard voices and shouted. They had to shout too, as the snow muffled our exchanges. They would have to set up a belay on buried skis back from the edge of the crevasse, then lower someone in to dig me out, with the rope engaged in a pulley system that would aid us both out of the crevasse. Adele later told me that Sven seemed shocked by the turn of events, so she had to take charge and lower Adam in, near to the spot from which my voice seemed to be coming.

Adam, confronted by this massive pile of snow, was somewhat nonplussed: 'Err, Dave, where are you? I don't know where to start.'

I took a deep breath, 'Try using your transceiver. That should help.'

'Right, yes, of course.' And that's exactly what he did.

As the weight of snow was lifted from my upper body, I was able to help, wrestling my head free with the help of my right arm, then both arms. My legs, however, remained trapped, and it took Adam more digging to free them. There was an enormous sense of relief when I could finally twist my legs, apparently undamaged, out of the packed snow.

Taking the skis off, I swung and flexed my limbs experimentally, braced for pain, but luckily with no ill effects, and had a chance to take in the situation. Adam and I were in a kind of bergschrund that stretched along the flank of the mountain, roofed by a snow ceiling, or at least it had been roofed until I'd crashed through it. To either side the tunnel stretched into darkness where a greater depth of snow still roofed it in. So *that* was the crevasse danger that the recommended route was designed to avoid.

Enough of the snow bridge had collapsed that in fact Adam and I could use our ice axes to climb out up a kind of ramp of snow blocks that it formed, belayed but without recourse to the pulley system, managed by Adele and Sven above.

'Well done all! You did a great job there,' I enthused, happy to be out.

'Yes, well, that's enough excitement for one day. I suppose we'd better get back to the hut,' Adele replied. 'Are you all right to ski?'

Perhaps it was the rush of adrenalin after escape from entombment, but I was having none of that. 'You've got to be joking! I'm not giving up on the mountain after falling into a crevasse trying to get up it! I reckon it's only another hour, tops. What do you reckon, lads?'

'Err, yeah, okay,' Adam mumbled with a look at his mum, but I could see Adele was coming round to the idea, if a bit surprised by my reaction. Sven was his usual phlegmatic self, but also agreed.

The route was rolling, skating the skis sometimes, stepping up, then letting them run, as well as skinning our way along the whaleback of the main ridge. Cloud hung about us, parting to give glimpses of other mountains in every direction as we descended. Despite my crevasse

Sorting ourselves out after the crevasse incident

burial, we all favoured skiing the north-east face at its least threatening point, one at a time. In descent, most crevasses collapse after they've been skied over; by the time they've been triggered, the skier is past. On this occasion none opened up, but we had decided to ski one at a time to allow space for evasive action. Superb powder snow took us down to the hut in fine style, with views of the mountains to the east opening up around us.

I'd started aching by the time we reached the hut, in places where the weight of snow blocks had struck me, so went for a lie-down on my bunk while Adele and Adam sorted out a meal. A few painkillers made for a suitably quiet night.

We rose to a cloudy day and set off for the Bow Hut in poor visibility, arriving just three hours later. Settling down to make a brew, I overheard a guy addressing a newly arrived Canadian team about some Brits he'd met on Mt Logan. That caught my attention.

'And a couple of these Brits went up too fast and one went blind with the altitude, had to be evacuated by helicopter.'

'Tim?' I called over. 'Tim Grey?'

He paused in his story. 'Dave? I don't believe this!'

'Yeah, I thought that story sounded familiar,' I said, laughing.

Bear hugs and handshakes later we were introducing our teams to each other.

'Where've you come from?' Tim asked.

'Peyto Hut. Skinned in across Peyto Lake the day before. We skied Mt Rhondda yesterday, and I fell in a crevasse.'

'Still crazy Brits then! The crevasse was bad luck, but that approach to Peyto Hut takes twice as long as the one to the Bow.'

'Well, we're trying to do the classic traverse from Peyto to West Louise Lodge. What about you? What are you doing here?'

'Just hanging out for a few days, looking at some big lines. We have some people crossing the Olive-Nicholas Col to find their way down those cliffs to the south of us later,' he pointed in the direction of St Nicholas Peak.

'Okay. Right. We'll watch out for them.'

With some brightness in the afternoon, I took Adele and Adam out to revise snow techniques and crevasse rescue more thoroughly. Yesterday's experience had increased my wariness about crevasses. Sven thought he knew enough, and stayed at the hut talking with some of Tim's team. Crowfoot Mountain opposite the hut on the other side of the cirque was looking good, but I was more interested in Mt Gordon, out of sight behind St Nicholas Peak; it would allow me to scout the start of the route to the next hut.

Back in the hut, Tim was talking on a two-way radio with some of his people out on the mountain. Several had made descents of the steep snows between rocks on the cliffs to the south between St Nicholas and Vulture Peaks, but more to skier's left where the angle was less extreme. Now a couple of guys were attempting to work out routes further to skier's right, on much steeper ground.

One was stopped at the head of a tongue of snow lolling down a buttress but running into rocks below. He was checking with Tim on the radio: 'No. No descent directly below. No way through. Repeat; no way down from where you are. You need to traverse skier's right...' Exciting stuff! The instructions went on, committing the skiers to improbable lines, but I'd worked out by then that they were very good skiers.

'They're going to come down a good way below the hut. Are you going to be able to see them?'

'It's safe enough down there, and they have radios. They'll probably ski all the way down into the bowl and then skin back up to the hut.'

It was especially cosy to bask before the log stove in the dining area as people trickled in from the hill and during the evening the stove in the dormitory was lit to raise the temperature before we settled down for the night. It was expected that visitors split kindling with axes left out by the pile of logs deposited by helicopter when the full barrels from the toilets were collected. This was a much more environmentally friendly system, unlike the long-drop loos still evident at huts in the Alps.

The following day Adele decided to take a day off while Sven, Adam and I made an ascent of Mt Gordon. In improving weather, Sven set a cracking pace and we reached the summit in 2 hours 40 minutes, well ahead of anyone else from the hut. At one point on the ascent, we had skirted a deep windscoop with its very own cornices next to a buttress of black rock holding snow on every ledge and in every crack. Cloud had continued to dominate, despite times when the sun glowed like a diffused globe of light that seemed only just above us, so there were no views from the summit. Vague dark buttresses and different shades of white where snow slopes changed angle were about all we could see.

In descent, visibility improved enough to get a good idea of the route to the col between Mt Olive and St Nicholas Peak which would be the first stage of our journey next day. The impressive pinnacle of St Nicholas Peak seen from the hut was now revealed to be the end of a ridge rising from the col. The light was a bit flat, but we skied down in more fantastic powder, and Sven decided to jump off a corniced ridge he had scoped out on the ascent, near a group of 13 skiers climbing up from the hut. Adam was also learning to relax into his skiing as the old skills returned thanks to the helpful snow conditions. Back at the hut, from late afternoon into the evening, the haze cleared to blue skies and fluffy clumps of cloud, with lovely light revealing the route back to the road and all the details of the mountains around us in the clear air.

Sven had been chatting animatedly with Tim's team rather than ours, perhaps because he identified with them as better skiers than us. They had plans to ski Mt Des Polius, about a 24 km round trip, and Sven wanted to join them: 'I know it's a long way, but I think I can branch off and cross the Olive-Nicholas Col to ski down to the Balfour Hut on the way back so I can join you to go over the Balfour Pass next day.' He was obviously keen.

'Okay Sven, I can see you want to have a go, but we can't wait for you at the Balfour Hut if you don't make it. Our bookings at the Scott Duncan Hut are only for one night, and there may be other teams going through taking up those bed spaces on subsequent nights. Plus, the weather situation may be too good for us to ignore or too bad for you to try to reach us if it turns during the day. Or you may simply be too tired for your plan. There's a lot of uncertainties there.'

Adam kept out of it, but Adele asked, 'Are you sure you want to do this? Even if it means you might not complete the traverse and you could be on your own in crevassed territory?'

'Yes, I'm sure,' Sven replied. 'Des Polius is not often done, and this is an opportunity.'

'Sure,' I said, 'but it's also an outside chance, and risks not doing what you came here for. Adele has a point about lone travel in this area, and I can't say I think it's a good idea. But I'm not your guide – we're just a 'bunch of mates' – and all I can do is advise against it, and understand if you choose not to take that advice. Sorry, but I need to make that clear with Adam and Adele witnessing it, because there have been legal actions in Canada and (who knows?) your family might decide to make a case against me if you're killed. In the end you're a responsible adult and it's your decision.'

'Okay. I understand, but I'm still going.'

'Right, so if you don't get to the Balfour Hut tomorrow, you do understand that we won't be waiting?'

'Yes.'

'Fine. Good luck!'

I also took the opportunity that evening to talk to the evident leaders of the team of 13 that I'd seen earlier out on the snow. They were a guide and an aspirant guide taking a team of students on an outdoor professional course who had chosen to specialise in ski mountaineering for three months. I think it was the course at Calgary University run by Murray Toft, who had published the Wapta Icefields map that we were using. They too were heading for the Balfour Hut on the next stage of the traverse in the morning.

Sven left early with Tim's team. Later, Adele, Adam and I skinned after them. With the trail broken and our lightened sacks, relieved of half our food rations, we made short work of the climb up to the Olive-Nicholas Col. There we stashed our excess baggage in a sheltered spot, reducing our rucksacks to day-sacks before climbing on foot, using crampons and ice axes, along the ridge to the summit of Mt Olive. There was a shoulder on the ridge from which skiers had left tracks of steep descents down to the Vulture Glacier, but we continued along the broadening ridge to the highest point.

Clouds mottled the surface of the Wapta Icefield and the peaks around it with dark patchwork patterns on the snow. Looking up, we saw those patterns were white and fluffy against blue sky above them, and we summitted in sunshine. The cornices to the east of the ridge outcropped in shelves, supported by snow buttresses beneath them but we steered well clear to avoid triggering any cornice collapse. Despite

the bubbling cloud, beyond a sawtooth arête cutting down to Vulture Col from the east ridge of Mt Gordon, we could see all the way to Mt Balfour and the route over the Balfour Pass that we needed to take next day. Which of the black dots in the snow below was the hut we couldn't tell at that distance.

In descent the narrowness of the ridge route to the north onto St Nicholas Peak's summit was very noticeable, and no one was attempting it, including us. Back at the col, we sorted out our kit for the ski down the Vulture Glacier. Skiing east first, towards Vulture Peak, I then bore south-east, before bearing south. Spotting the Balfour Hut, we took a final swing east to the door. The outdoor education team had already arrived, having not climbed Mt Olive, so their tracks had been an aid to our navigation, but I couldn't help noticing that if Sven joined us the hut would have been overbooked. When I mentioned it to the guide, he had to confess that they had included extra people in their team beyond their original booking. No harm done there, but at the smaller Scott Duncan Hut, which theoretically only slept 12, there was going to be pressure on stove use and very cramped bunk space.

The crux of the traverse lay ahead, but the route looked almost amenable, illuminated by bright afternoon sunshine, despite billowing clouds casting shadows over the hut itself. Despite the clearance there was no sign of Sven then or later that day. We had no choice but to go on without him, hoping his no-show did not indicate anything more serious than a change of plan.

It was a different story in the morning. There had been snowfall overnight, and it was still snowing and blowing. After some debate, the team of 13 decided to go for it.

But with Adele and Adam's lack of experience in alpine conditions, I had some reservations about continuing with them, despite a full quota of GPS waypoints for the route, so I had a word with the other team's guide: 'I can see you're going on despite the weather, and I was thinking of following in your tracks. We'd be operating independently, but there's no doubt that having you ahead would be helpful; I mean, you must have done this route lots of times. Is that going to be a problem for you?'

The guide called the aspirant over, and they considered for a few moments, then decided. 'No, I don't think so. You're pretty experienced and if we all stay close together and follow the tracks, there shouldn't be much risk of you guys going into a crevasse.'

'Okay. Thanks. I've got a set of GPS waypoints, so will be able to check how the route is going from the rear.' I didn't mention my crevasse burial. There may have been a little guilt about overbooking involved in their decision, but turning us down would have solved that problem for them in the Scott Duncan Hut, so I appreciated their generosity.

The route made an ascending traverse from Balfour Pass towards a Black Cliff also known as the Nunatak. Much of that traverse and the climb around the Black Cliff was threatened by unstable seracs breaking away from the ice cliffs on Mt Balfour's north-east face. An upper ramp was more threatened, but the lower ramp separated by a shallower band of seracs meant climbing around the Black Cliff through steep and seriously crevassed territory. The outdoor team skied down to the right slightly from the hut, to reach the foot of the glacier, and my team followed as the others swung left, climbing steeply up the lower ramp to reach the Nunatak.

The early start had contributed to the gloom that surrounded us, with vague masses of ice looming to our right, but as we climbed there were times when cloud thinned and the sun broke through, spotlighting our surroundings in sudden detail. Slowly, steadily, we gained height on snow ramps through crevasses, twisted and broken against the solid rock of the Black Cliff, their depths obscured by drifted snow that somehow made them more menacing. Emerging above the cliff took us nearer to the ice cliffs to our right, towering above us but mercifully frozen into immobility thanks to the storm.

At about 2850m, the steepness was lost in an expansive snowfield below the south-east ridge of Mt Balfour, so the guides took bearings for the pass about a kilometre away, where the ridge declined to a kind of shoulder that was Balfour High Pass, before rising and narrowing on its way to the steep little summit of Lilliput Mountain. Reaching the pass, the whole team stopped to toast our success with whatever our flasks contained and chunks of chocolate. Skins were stripped from our skis and bindings locked for the ski down to the Scott Duncan Hut. In the lee of the pass it was calm, but I could tell from the sheets of snow being wind-driven over our heads that a hard time lay ahead.

Crossing High Balfour Pass, we dropped into the full force of the storm in what was close to a complete whiteout. Skiing east meant that occasional glimpses of the ridge leading to Lilliput Mountain could act as a navigation handrail, but we were reliant on GPS waypoints to decide when to swing south towards Mt Daly and the hut. Through ski goggles spattered with snow, each of us desperately tried to keep up with the skier ahead, unconsciously adapting to the nature of the terrain indicated by their movements, and with little else visible around us. My hands and feet were becoming numb as I held to the line of the descent, but without enough exertion to generate much heat in icy gusts of wind that threatened to blow us off our skis. Suddenly there were other figures beyond the one in front; all stopped, and I could see the guides in the lead beginning to take off their skis.

The Scott Duncan Hut is perched on a spur of Mt Daly above the glacier, usually accessed by a rising traverse from the north-east, but that would have involved stopping and fixing skins again – a risky business in that storm. Instead, the guides had wisely opted to ski directly across the glacier towards the waypoint that marked the hut, then bootpack up the slope below it, a climb of around 100m. It was one way of warming us up before entering the hut.

Following the tracks of the person ahead, and carrying skis, each of us toiled up to stash our skis outside the hut and crash inside, scattering snow all over the floor. Unlike the other huts, this one had no outer door and anteroom to keep out the wind and offer a place to brush snow from clothes and boots before entering through the inner door. We were to paddle about in melted snow for the entire time that we were there.

With 16 of us in a hut intended for 12, with only four gas rings and one sink, we just had to retire to the communal bunk-shelves and take turns to sort out food and drink. Fortunately, my team was equipped with cook-in-the-bag meals, so we only needed boiling water to add to the bags. The Canadians had more complex culinary needs. Windows and walls were soon running with condensation, and more snow was carried in on boots or blew in through the door every time someone went out to the toilet or to collect fresh snow for melting. There were times when the floor was awash, but at least we had refuge from the storm.

Packed in on the two bunk-shelves, we found it a warm enough night despite the damp, but needed to rise early to get everyone through breakfast to leave at 7 am. With such heavy snowfall, the avalanche risk of the descent route would be high. There was little change in the weather, but none of us wanted to wait it out at the hut. In deep snow, we slid slowly down to the glacier then skinned across to the pass between Mt Daly and Mt Niles, looming above us on either side as we passed to the right of the little peak in the centre of the pass.

Beyond, the slope steepened and clearly posed an avalanche danger. The guides conferred, then one, still with his skins on, broke a trail at an easy angle across the slope to the right, telling us to follow him exactly in the track, one by one, but only when he signalled to do so. Eventually his signal came and the first skier followed. Once we had regrouped it was possible to continue traversing very carefully across less steep slopes out onto a shoulder of more rolling terrain where poling was sometimes necessary, before skiing around to forested slopes above Sherbrooke Creek.

There was some fun tree-skiing down the drainage to the creek; so much fun that the Canadian team decided to skin back up and make further descents, yo-yoing the powder. Visibility had improved as we descended, and I suspect it was the relief of moving into safer territory that encouraged the yo-yoing, but my team expressed their relief in voting to get down before any deterioration in the weather set in.

Following Sherbrooke Creek was something of a roller-coaster ride around some meandering in the watercourse that created ups and downs over little spurs requiring us to keep up momentum to cover the ground. I skied onto a convenient rise at several points to wait for Adele and Adam, but on one occasion they didn't appear and there seemed to be some shouting back up the track. We tried to communicate, but couldn't hear the words of each other's shouts – as I made preparations to skin back up to help, to my relief they appeared. Adele had taken a fall near the stream. She had saved herself by grabbing a convenient sapling but was poised above the water, unable to let go without ending up in the creek. Fortunately, Adam was able get off his skis and heave her out of danger. The incident revealed how easy it was to lose touch with each other when slaloming through trees along a stream bed, and I stopped to regroup more frequently after that.

Where the creek dropped over a waterfall we branched right to descend steeply through trees, slowed nicely by the depth of snow, then skied more easily down to Sherbrooke Lake. Snow had been falling the whole time, and the surrounding pines were laden with its burden, but the lake was frozen hard enough for us to cross it confidently. The summits were all hidden by cloud, but the extraordinary flatness of the lake bordered by the density of the pines struck me with its strangeness after so much time amongst snowy peaks in the icefields. On the southern shore we branched off left, climbing up through trees to find the waymarked summer trail. It was well signed, but winter storms had felled trees, creating an obstacle course that made for a wild ride down to West Louise Lodge.

At the road, steel bins, gravel heaps and mud felt like a different world, but the lodge was open for us to wait in shelter for our taxi to arrive. The 'Lucky 13' arrived just before we left, and I had time to thank the guides for their efforts. Back at Lake Louise Youth Hostel, we found Sven alive and well. They hadn't managed to climb Mt Des Polius and, with bad weather forecast, he had skied out from the Bow Hut to the road with Tim's team. He was heading off to Banff, but

Adam stayed over with Adele and me, cooking a fine meal for us all in the hostel kitchen. A family of Canadian skiers told us that evening that they had made four attempts at the Wapta Icefields traverse without success, but were still determined to try it again.

2016

The 2006 trip had been a great experience, and then in 2016 the Alpine Club of Canada opened the first new hut for decades. The Richard and Louise Guy Hut was built on a col north of Yoho Peak to enable ski mountaineers to make an east–west traverse of the Wapta Icefields from the Bow Hut to link with the Stanley Mitchell Hut. Susie Amann and Jack Waters proposed to jointly lead a trip for the Eagle Ski Club to make that crossing during the Christmas–New Year holiday in 2016–17, and I signed up for it, along with four others – strength in numbers!

Skinning up to the Bow Hut from Num-ti-Jah Lodge on Christmas Eve in temperatures of -20°C was a shock to the system, and the hut was no warmer. Though we made sterling efforts to get the stoves going, frozen wood didn't catch light easily or burn well, and one person's idea of a firelighter was a candle stump but we survived!

Christmas Day brought clear skies and sunshine as we climbed out of the shadow of St Nicholas Peak, heading across the glacier to Mt Gordon for a shake-down tour. All wrapped up against the cold, Griff reported skinning in two layers of down without breaking sweat, but there was concern about numb hands and feet from others, including me. We topped out in the clearest conditions I've ever seen in Canada; an extensive panorama of snow peaks stretching for miles in all directions, emphasising the wilderness surrounding us. Across the Yoho Glacier to the west, we could see the Guy Hut, a dot on the ridge between Yoho Peak and Mt Collie. It seemed a long way off. The cold meant that we didn't linger, but instead linked patches of soft snow for a brilliant descent. It was great way to spend Christmas Day, and there were even celebratory nips of whisky to warm us up back at the Bow Hut.

On Boxing Day, the plan was to traverse to the Guy Hut. Fully loaded, we skinned up past St Nicholas Peak, heading for the gap that

Crossing the Wapta Icefield towards Mt Gordon

would take us onto the Yoho Glacier. The sky was brilliantly clear, but a cold wind blew viciously into our faces. Windchill must have been taking temperatures down below -30°C. My hands and feet grew colder despite the exertion of climbing, and I became increasingly doubtful about continuing.

When Susie stopped to take a bearing, we huddled together and I voiced my concerns: 'I'm beginning to doubt the wisdom of continuing with this.'

'Me too,' Griff responded.

'What do others think?' Susie asked.

'I'm feeling okay, and I think we should just get our heads down and get on with it.' Megan was a very fit young lass, and keen with it.

'Okay. It's not that we can't physically go on, but in these temperatures we're dangerously close to the edge. If someone went into a crevasse and broke a leg, for example, that could be a death sentence, and not only for the casualty. Spending time winching someone out of a crevasse and

Summit of Mt Gordon, Christmas Day

tending to them can take ages, and we could see others going down with hypothermia.' I was thinking aloud, but my views were hardening.

Others chipped in with similar misgivings, and we reached a group decision to return to the hut and hope for better conditions next morning. It would mean giving up a mountain day at the Guy Hut, but better that than risk anyone's life.

Back at the hut a couple had arrived to simply spend a night at a hut in winter and hopefully get some glacier skiing, but they had no news of better weather. The following morning the wind had not abated, and visibility had deteriorated. There was tacit agreement that we should make another attempt to see if it cleared, but when I stepped outside it seemed that the strength of the wind had redoubled and it was obvious to me that conditions were getting worse.

'No. I don't see the point,' I said to myself and then repeated to Susie. 'I'm not going. This is not better than yesterday. It's worse. I'll ski out to the road and get a ride to the youth hostel. I can hire a car and do some day tours from the valley, weather permitting, and meet you at the hostel when you get down. There're no crevasses on the descent, and I'll ski very carefully.'

It was difficult to tell if anyone else was wavering, but I'd made my decision and had no regrets as they skinned off into the wind and cloud. Back inside, the couple came over to check out my intentions and asked if they could ski down with me as conditions were so bad. That would be useful for all three of us, so I readily agreed. The ski out was uneventful with improving visibility as we lost height, although it was obvious that the exposed side of the valley was being swept clear of snow by the wind. Looking back up the canyon, I could see a tumult of cloud and spindrift hiding the sun.

I booked into the youth hostel to find myself sharing a room with two Americans who had no intention of obeying the rules against eating and drinking in the dorms, so I left them scattering crisps and crumbs and retired to the upstairs lounge with my guidebook. Not long into reading up on day routes from the road, I was aware of other arrivals. The rest of the team had also returned.

Conditions had indeed been worse; bad enough to turn them around again, and when they reached the Bow Hut, a family group, up for some powder skiing, had reported a bad weather forecast for the next few days. That was enough for them to pull the plug on any further plans for the traverse. Instead, we had a day at Kicking Horse Resort, making some good descents of chutes from the summit, another day at Rogers Pass sampling some great tree-skiing, and more days of glade skiing from the road. The trip had been a reminder of the extreme cold that can be experienced in the depths of a Canadian winter, and just how serious conditions can get in the Wapta Icefields, but I still hankered after that east–west traverse.

2019

In 2018 I'd planned a sail and ski trip to Iceland, but the cost, post-Brexit, proved prohibitive. When I cancelled, other interested parties had simply made other arrangements, but my Spanish friend, Almudena, just asked, 'Where are we going instead, then?' She'd never been to

Entering the ice cave beneath the glacier

Canada, so it seemed an obvious choice, particularly as it would allow me to test-drive my back with medium-weight load-carrying after recovering from a spinal injury. We booked nearly three weeks in late April–early May.

The plan to base ourselves in Canmore for some warm-up tours was frustrated by a lack of snow despite the abnormally low temperatures for late April, so we decamped to Lake Louise, where conditions were not much better but at least allowed us to get onto north-facing slopes and make some turns through the trees. Then it was time to start the east–west traverse, skinning across Bow Lake from the parking lot, along the drainage, and over a spur to reach the canyon that led to the cirque below the Bow Hut.

The plan had been to skin over to the Guy Hut and on to the Stanley Mitchell Hut, hoping to ski mountains like Collie, Des Polius and McArthur on the way. This was soon abandoned in the face of days of powerful winds, poor visibility and snowfall. We stayed on at

Climbing St Nicholas Peak

the Bow Hut, skiing some fine powder on the glacier, exploring a remarkable ice cave under the snout of the glacier, making a circuit of St Nicholas Peak and skiing Mt Rhondda. Standing in the ice cave, it was very strange to think of all that tonnage of ice over our heads.

As we were coming to the end of our booking at the ACC huts without having got further than the first one, a day dawned with sunshine and less wind, despite the apparently inevitable cloud. Out early, we skinned easily to the summit of Mt Gordon, this time completely windless, with great views of the distant Guy Hut and Mt Balfour. In descent, instead of skiing the line of ascent, I found perfect champagne powder working skier's right towards the east face, hung with seracs. Probing the icefalls with little descents and traverses, I found a way through to the right of them, straight down onto the glacier within striking distance of Vulture Col. It was a brilliant steep powder run, ending in a long schuss across the glacier before refixing skins to climb up to the St Nicholas–Mt Olive Col. 'Crazy!' Almudena commented – but she doesn't have to deal with crevasses and seracs in the Pyrenees.

The weather was holding, and nothing like as windy as on previous days. It might have been a good day to go to the Guy Hut, but with bad weather forecast to follow, we could have been trapped there as our food ran out. We stripped skins, snacked and contemplated the long thin ridge to the summit of St Nicholas Peak. There was a residual track, but no one had been up there recently. Skiing over for a better look, I could tell we were both tempted, so I dug a snow pit for our excess kit to deter any investigations by the ravens that were loitering hopefully nearby. Then, with crampons and ice axes, we went to have a look.

Almudena led off, but I caught up with her where she was hesitating about the line to take ahead. I led a traverse below the crest that solved the problem, then kicked steps on up the ridge. The climbing was remarkably exposed, with rocky drops to the west and a snow face sweeping away to the east, but very straightforward until we came to a 5-metre pitch of ice and loose rock, just off vertical. That was more technical, but gave access to the narrow summit platform with panoramic views over the surrounding icefields. After the obligatory photos, I climbed down and braced myself to break Almudena's fall if she slipped on descending the tricky step. Then we reversed the route along the ridge, which was just as impressive in descent.

Back at the skis, I persuaded Almudena to ski north-east from the col beneath the east face of St Nicholas, more or less directly to the hut. After a fast run to the steepening, I made sure we were avoiding rocky cliffs to our right, then dropped onto the steep snows that fell in steps to the foot of the glacier. On the lips of the steps there were outcrops of rock and ice offering islands of safety from which to work out the line down the next steep pitch below. The powder was perfect, at least until we reached patches of sun-warmed snow when we were skiing down shallower slopes to the hut. Looking back at our tracks threading their way improbably down the face above the hut was a perfect end to a fantastic day out.

The hut had been quite crowded over the Easter weekend, but became less so afterwards. Most of the visitors shared my surprise at the conditions, one stating, 'I was expecting spring snow, not powder!' More days of bad weather validated our decision not to get trapped in the Guy Hut. It was disappointing, but there were compensations in the form of great powder runs on the glacier above the hut.

Descending the steep final pitch from the summit of St Nicholas Peak

Then it was the last day of our booking. Almudena and I skied a couple of laps of the glacier before descending from the hut, using the ascent tracks of a team of four who had arrived as we left in deteriorating weather. The navigation was fine right down to the shore of Bow Lake, whereupon the storm closed in and I lost sight of Num-ti-jah Lodge on the further shore. In the whiteout I must have trended to the left, and when the margin of the lake came into view, I was in danger of breaking through melting ice into the shallows. These were nervous moments before Almudena spotted vague signs of a track to the right, and we followed them to the safety of the lodge trail.

A few rest days were planned, but neither of us could resist the good weather on the second. A day trip took us onto the Saddleback Trail for a circuit of Mt Fairview. Crossing Surprise Pass, we found the steepness of the descent as much of a surprise as the good quality of the powder. Skating our skis back across a completely frozen Lake Louise amongst crowds of ice-walkers was a marked contrast to the sense of remoteness in the deserted Sheol Valley before the lonely climb to Surprise Pass.

Glacier skiing below St Nicholas Peak

Then on 2 May, we were back at Bow Lake to take up our bookings for the north–south traverse. I planned to traverse over from the Bow to the Peyto Hut for a couple of days peak-bagging, but bad weather saw us wandering uncertainly in the 'White Room' somewhere near Mt Baker, before giving up and returning to a hut that was bitterly cold with only the two of us in residence and no stove to heat the place.

Then on a beautifully clear day, we headed directly for the Balfour Hut via the Olive-Nicholas Col. The empty open glacier reminded me of Antarctica, as slowly the tip of Mt Olive and then that of St Nicholas Peak rose above a snow horizon; but as the mountains bulked larger, Mt Olive was obscured by a bank of low-lying mist that hung less densely on St Nicholas Peak. As we neared the col the mist cleared, and tracks and distant figures appeared, three climbing the north-west ridge of Mt Olive with skis on their backs. Mist closed in again on reaching the col, so I gave up any thoughts of climbing Mt Olive in favour of descent to the Balfour Hut before any worse weather came in. As we started that descent, sudden snowfall and swirling cloud

Approaching Olive-Nicholas Col, with climbers on the ridge

swept in, so I headed east to pick up the handrail which the south ridge of Vulture Peak offered, bounding the glacier on its east side.

Skiing down the Vulture Glacier allowed us some nice turns as the visibility improved, but on nearing the hut we had to backtrack and go around at times, finding the way barred by low cliffs in the moraine. I didn't remember those being there 13 years earlier. The GPS and tracks of an earlier party finally took us to the Balfour Hut in much improved weather, though I was puzzled by a woman who stepped out of the door shouted 'Welcome!' then disappeared inside again. This was our first contact with 'the Crazy Canadians', as Almudena later described them.

As we were sorting out our skis, Ken Belanger, a guide, arrived with two clients, Stan and Sandy. Ken seemed to be known to the other team of five Canadians, from another life, and knew Owen Day, another Canadian guide and mutual friend who had relocated to London. We all got on well once inside, and Almudena told them about how we had come to be there, and some of our previous adventures. They were

Climbing past the Nunatak on the way to Balfour High Col

somewhat surprised that I was taking on a trip of this seriousness in my sixties.

That evening, after brewing and eating, to my surprise, I found my low-status Black Country accent in demand on account of its 'Britishness.' They wanted me to read them a bed-time story! To be specific, a chapter from Game of Thrones which one of the clients had on the Kindle app of his phone. It took all my years of teaching English to manage such an unprepared reading, but I was even prevailed upon for a second chapter before lights-out!

The night had been cold with a skyful of glittering stars when I made my last visit to the outside toilet, but light snowfall greeted us in the morning. Ken's team led off with the Canadians, led by Jim, following and Almudena and I bringing up the rear, this time skiing directly down to the foot of the glacial slope to ascend a steeper diagonal traverse towards the Nunatak. Ken was trailing a probe to check out any suspicious crevasses, confident enough to leave the rope in Sandy's rucksack. The rest of us didn't share that confidence and roped up after crossing a precarious snow bridge over one crevasse. There were plenty of other crevasses around but most were advertising their presence.

It was great to be able to see clearly the terrain that I had moved through in wind and snow on the previous occasion although the ice cliffs balanced above rock outcrops and twisted crevasses were definitely more intimidating seen in all their savage detail. Cloud rolled in as we gathered at High Balfour Pass, and lingered long enough for all three teams to give up on any idea of climbing Mt Balfour. The tension was eased by clowning from the Canadians, striking exaggerated poses with the inevitable victory V-signs for photos. Almudena soon got into the mood and gesticulated with the best of them, though I steadfastly maintained my British reserve.

Visibility improved for some nice turns skiing down the glacier so Ken decided to give his clients a consolation prize by climbing Lilliput Mountain. Almudena and I followed, and we all topped out within minutes of each other. There was some steep skiing off the summit and down the ridge to a corniced saddle, from which we could look down towards the cliffs and canyon of Balfour Creek drainage. Jim's team had arrived there by then, and skinned on up to the summit while we skied back down to the glacier.

Back at the gear cache buried in the snow, we reloaded our rucksacks as the skies cleared to show the cliffs of Lilliput Mountain with the tiny colourful figures of Jim's team on the very top against a bright blue patch of sky. Skiing off in a south-easterly arc, we reached a point where we needed to fix skins before swinging west to slant up the spur on which the Scott Duncan Hut was located. I glanced back to see the sawtooth rock pinnacles of Lilliput's south ridge against that same blue sky, and felt a momentary pang of regret that we had not attempted Mt Balfour. Then I skinned on after Ken's team, now dwarfed by the bulk of Mt Daly above them.

The hut was just the same as it had been in 2006; no porch, limited cookers and a pervading dampness. With fewer of us in occupancy, the floor stayed relatively dry and it was easier to take turns cooking and washing up, but we all agreed that the place could use a little TLC. So could I after discovering that my last dehydrated expedition meal was inedible, despite being well within its use by date. Almudena shared some of her couscous, and the Canadians donated chocolate in return for

Skinning beneath the seracs on the east face of Mt Balfour

another two-chapter reading exploring some pretty dark territory of the imagination in Game of Thrones. Afterwards, Marlies told me discreetly that she thought Ken had been a little choked by the reading. It was nice to have an appreciative audience, and I think any concerns that my age might be problem were allayed after skiing with me that day.

At 7 am we made an early start to be sure of crossing Sherbrooke Lake safely before the afternoon sun reached the ice. All of us chose our own more or less steep descent from the hut, schussing until the slope brought us to a halt, then transitioning to skins for the traverse south to the Daly–Niles pass, again passing to the right of the Nipple in the centre. From the pass a descent and short skinned ascent took us onto a shoulder below the south ridge of Mt Niles. Terah, the quietest of the women, seemed to be tinkering with her bindings but said nothing as I waited then skinned past, assuming it was just a minor hitch. At the shoulder there was more posing and victory signs as we switched

Weather closing in on the recommended approach to the Scott Duncan Hut,
near the foot of the spur on the right

to downhill mode. There had been distant blue patches of sky at the
pass but now cloud was gathering about the peaks to the south that
reared above the forested valley slopes like shark's teeth; views that had
been lost to me in the storm of 2006.

Unfortunately, it turned out that Terah was having a more serious
problem clearing ice from one binding that just kept releasing, so I
should have checked her situation more thoroughly and offered
assistance. Instead, the rest of us waited and worried until she appeared.
I guess Jim also thought I should have been more considerate as back
marker, so asked Almudena and me to go on ahead, although Marlies
suggested, 'Take no notice.'

I thought we could probably lead off but still keep in touch, so
Almudena and I skied rapidly south beneath the cornices of the south
ridge of Mt Niles, swinging around the blunt nose of it and down
towards the trees above Upper Sherbrooke Creek. There seemed to be
a clearing descending through the forest with ski tracks in the snow
– but was it the right line?

The Canadians caught up as I dithered.

'There are tracks but I don't have a GPS waypoint? Do you?' I asked.

'Yes, I've got a point to turn down towards the creek, but I think it's 100 metres or so further west.'

'Well perhaps these tracks go down to join that descent,' I said. 'There aren't any signs of anyone skinning back up, so there must be a way through.' I suppose I was asserting our independence. There was no crevasse danger at this point, and I didn't want Jim to feel any responsibility for us.

'I reckon we'll just ski through these trees a little further, and see what we find at the waypoint.'

'Okay, but I think we'll go down here and see you later.' I looked to Almudena for assent and she nodded, so off we went for some fine tree-skiing in softening spring snow.

I was right about there being no tracks coming up, but the trees became denser, the snow cruddier, and the angle of the slope steeper. Instead of going right, the tracks had taken us left, and I came to an abrupt halt at the brink of some buttresses. Patchy signs of tracks seemed to be traversing skier's left above the drop, so I broke trail in that direction towards what I thought was a small creek-bed, clear of trees, that looked as though it would lead down to a junction with Sherbrooke Creek. The traverse involved forcing our way through low branches of the pines and avoiding sliding into tree wells around the bigger trees where snow shed from the branches had built a sort of pit surrounding the trunk.

The descent into the little creek's drainage was steep and technical owing to the boulders outcropping from the slope and there was one occasion when I paused for Almudena to follow my tracks, but there was no sign of her for long enough to alarm me. There was no response to my shouts, but just as I was about to bootpack up the slope she appeared. A tree-well had snared her and muffled her replies.

The bouldery creek-bed continued technical but the snow, shaded from the sun, was so much better that we found it fun. Breaking out onto the course of Sherbrooke Creek, we could see fresh tracks, making it clear that the Canadians were ahead of us, crossing and recrossing the snow-covered creek itself for the best line of descent. The sun broke through at times as we continued swinging turns around and over lumps and bumps, before descending the steep narrow trail through denser trees that bypassed the waterfall in the main creek-bed. Then Sherbrooke Lake lay before us, with the Canadians just entering the trees on the further shore. Looking back, we could see the rocky tower of Mt Niles dominating the valley we had descended.

Skating past a patch of open water, seamed with fallen trees, we freed our heels and continued sliding and skating across the snowy ice. Big rock faces around the lake totally validated the naming of this range as the Rocky Mountains. Gaining the southern shore led to more skating and a lot of stepping up to find the summer trail. At this point, both of us heard a few resounding whistles, and I was concerned that it might be someone in distress. The sound was just like the old school whistles – Acme Thunderers, I think they were called – but neither of us could identify the source, or any evidence that there was a problem for anyone. No one answered our shouts.

There was a thaw in progress, and after pushing the ski descent to its limit we were forced to strap our skis to our rucksacks for the final kilometre down to what was now named the Great Divide Lodge.

The Canadians were waiting to welcome us. Ken greeted me with a handshake and, 'Well done, Dave!' while Almudena was waving victory signs with her free hand and telling them she was 'Over the moon!' There were lots of photos taken, including one whole group selfie by Marlies showing ten smiling faces. Jim kindly drove Almudena and me back to the parking lot at Num-ti-jah Lodge, as they had another vehicle to collect, and from there, Ken, Sandy and Stan headed off to Jasper. The rest of us reassembled at Peyto's Café in Lake Louise for a large and very welcome lunch. Afterwards, as they dispersed to drive home, Marlies' parting comment was, 'I still can't believe you're doing this sort of thing at your age!'

I looked at Almudena. 'Just crazy, I guess,' I said, and laughed.

In a way it was ironic that I had teamed up with locals on both of the Wapta traverses despite the relatively tiny numbers of ski-mountaineers in the area, compared to the crowds found in huts in the Alps where, although there might be lots of people on the same route, I had rarely found any sense of teamwork. I'd still like to make the east-west traverse of the Wapta Icefields.

During other visits to Canada, I completed a 14-day Franklin Traverse in the Coast Range of British Columbia, but was forced to abandon the Bugaboos to Rogers Pass Traverse, in severe avalanche conditions, diverting to a less committing tour on the Drummond Icefield. We saw no other person most of the time, but were operating as an experienced team of ski-mountaineers. These were full-on expeditions travelling through a pristine environment, camping in the snow, carrying everything we needed in rucksacks and haul-bags, and making first tracks on mountains that might not have been skied for years; self-reliant, multi-day ski adventures!

***

Wikiloc | Wapta Traverse Trail after the Scott Duncan Hut the track diverts from the classic route down the Sherbrooke Valley to the Bath Glacier finish but the features remain on the map and *Wikiloc | Wapta traverse in summer Trail* shows the track of the classic route.

Also *waptaguidemap.jpg (1072×1615)* is online, sourced from *Summits and Icefields* by Chic Scott & Mark Klassen which is an invaluable planning guide.

https://www.wikiloc.com/back-country-skiing-trails/wapta-traverse-4178215#wp-4178219 (see Maps & QR Codes p.229)

EXPLORATORY EXPEDITIONS – KYRGYZSTAN

The Wapta Traverses in Canada are examples of committing expeditionary ski mountaineering in areas where glacial features and inevitable erosion can challenge expectations but the route and the mountains are still known factors. To take adventure skiing a step further means moving into terrain where no one has skied before. There is tremendous satisfaction in researching such a project to establish a game plan, and then testing it against the realities in the field. There's also the satisfaction of making first ascents of unclimbed peaks and ski descents that have never been skied, but exploration offers something more.

At the time of writing, I'm one of just 25 British mountaineers who have climbed all 52 of the independent 4000m mountains of the Alps, but it was a team effort involving a number of climbing and skiing partners. Moreover, after I'd written the book, *4000m: Climbing the Highest Mountains of the Alps,* and lectured on the subject, I was very aware of much common ground with the audience, the readership. Every audience that I addressed included at least one other person who had climbed a 4000m Alpine peak, and the feeling was one of shared celebration, not any sense of elitism. I also tried to make available in the book answers to those questions that had arisen while I was climbing those peaks but which I had never had the time to research sufficiently to answer at the time. Questions like: 'Why are Alpine maps so variable in quality?' and 'How did skiing come to the Alps?' The book became a sharing of learning as well as experiences. I felt like I was putting something back into alpinism. It's the antithesis of 'bragging rights' secured by purchasing an Everest ascent on the backs of the Sherpas.

Cutting edge mountaineering has become focused on hard ascents by career athletes, and good luck to them; but few of their climbs are ever repeated. With so many other virgin peaks to choose from in a remote area, why would anyone make a second ascent of a route? In the Alps a new route would be bound to be climbed and the details and grading verified, but that's far from the norm in the Greater Ranges. Hard new routes are tremendous personal achievements, but have come to be dominated by driven climbers who have been in danger of climbing themselves into extinction.

They may be an example to a few youngsters who might be inspired to push themselves harder to achieve harder routes, but the death of Tom Ballard and others like him is an indication of where that may lead. Extreme climbers are sometimes regarded as heroes, but it is worth remembering that heroes, as defined by the heroic societies from which they sprang, have been the champions of those communities who made sacrifices for their communities. Beowulf is the young hard-case who kills both Grendel and Grendel's monstrous mother, ending their reign of terror, but he is also the ageing ruler who must go out to kill the dragon, knowing it is likely to mean that he too will die. Unlike UK rock climbers who develop crags with new routes that other climbers can enjoy, exploratory mountaineers put little back into that climbing community comprising the majority of climbers who enjoy their mountaineering in whatever areas they can access at whatever level they choose to manage.

The exceptions are when new routes draw attention to new areas for climbing at various levels of difficulty, allowing others in the climbing community to explore the potential of those areas, but routes don't have to be hard to do that. Tom Nakamura's 13 years comprising 25 journeys into the mountains of east and south-east Tibet provided a framework for future adventures in those mountains, though he made few ascents in those years. The record of those travels in his books and editions of the *Japanese Alpine News* meant that others could follow, making subsequent ascents that indicated the quality of the climbing, and encouraged further exploration and mountaineering. I was one of those others.

It's not just the climbing community that can benefit from exploration. Communities based in remote areas can benefit from sensitive economic development that does not undermine their traditional values. The film *Sherpa* explores what happens when insensitive exploitation is thrown into sharp focus by horrific accidents on Everest; the 'smiling helpful Sherpas' are unsurprisingly less smiling and helpful when 16 of them die in a single avalanche. In contrast, in Kyrgyzstan local snow leopard hunters have found that they can make more money by guiding tourists to view and photograph the big cats than they could make from the skin of one; a win–win situation for the environment.

The personal satisfaction for an explorer who climbs or skis a new line is not diminished but enhanced by the knowledge that they are trail-blazing for others and thereby benefiting the local community but hopefully not overwhelming it. I found that experience in four expeditions to Kyrgyzstan, which for me were the ultimate skiing adventures.

***

The Kyrgyz Expeditions were from the outset very much an Eagle Ski Club (ESC) initiative. In 1998 Chris Watkins proposed a three-week expedition into the Tien Shan for the 1999 tour programme. Plans were based on her research whilst working in Kyrgyzstan and would have involved the hire of a helicopter to set up a base camp in the heart of the Ak-Shirak range, although she planned to ski out at the end of the trip. I believe there were only two helicopters that operated in the country at the time, and the army had first call on them. Money talks, however, so if people could commit to pay the helicopter charge in advance, then the trip would go ahead. There was a lot of interest but ultimately Chris was unable to secure the numbers required and the project folded.

Mountaineering in the Soviet Union used to be a competitive business, with climbs awarded points for seriousness and difficulty. Summer Camps were the focus for competitions in areas like the Caucasus and Pamirs, where most of the development took place. Young climbers were supported to attend such camps, and in a spirit of internationalism invitations were also extended to other countries, including the UK although the government was usually boycotting the USSR for one reason or another. Some enterprising individual UK climbers took up the offers turned down by the BMC and had a great time! A Czech climber once told me that during the Soviet era he had been able to travel and climb in places he could never have afforded to visit after independence.

In Kyrgyzstan, the main focus had been the high Pamirs; Pik Lenin, Khan Tengri, Pobeda, with the Snow Leopard Award for those who climbed the five 7000m peaks, including Pik Communism and Pik Korzhenevskaya in Tajikistan. There had also been a lot of development, even huts, in the Ala Archa range close to the capital, Bishkek, for the simple reason that it was so accessible from the main population centre in the country. All this had passed the Ak-Shirak range by. It was neither hard enough, nor high enough nor convenient enough to attract interest, and therefore proved to be fertile ground for first ascents on ski.

8

AK-SHIRAK 2003 –
A RECONNAISSANCE

In 2001 Steve Wright picked up the baton and gave advance notice of an expedition to the Tien Shan in 2003, with the promise of further details in 2002. Essentially, he was testing the level of interest and looking at ways to avoid the expense of helicopter access. He was also able to contact John Turk and Harry Locke, who had both been in the area with students in summer. In 2002 the details emerged, with the proposal to traverse the range via the Kara Say and Petrov glaciers, climbing significant mountains en route.

One of the biggest problems with expedition skiing is getting access to the mountains when the approach roads are all too often impassable under metres of snow. This time, although access would be up the Barskoon Gorge via the road to the Kumtor gold mine, kept open so that mining could continue throughout the winter, the expedition would have to cross the Suek Pass in order to reach the Kara Say Valley to the south of the range, and as the pass was not on the route to the gold mine it could be blocked by snow. So it was decided that if the pass did turn out to be blocked, access to the range would be attempted via one of the glaciers flowing north towards the mine access road.

It was at that point that I signed up for the trip and became involved in the ongoing evolution of that plan. An ESC member who was heli-skiing in the country reported high avalanche danger in March,

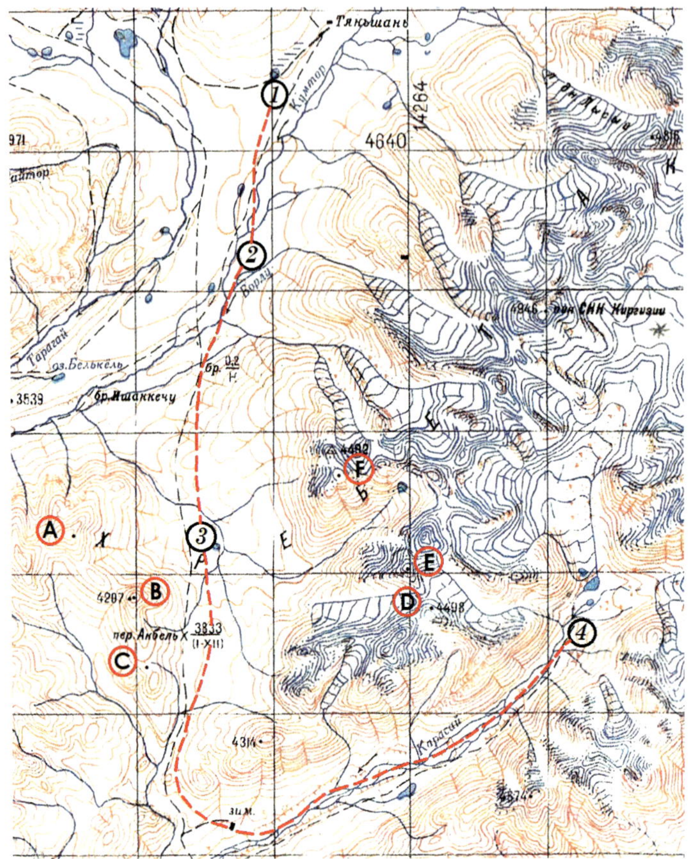

Ak-Shirak route map, 2003. Camps 1-4, Peaks A - F

our planned date for departure, and his guide had suggested May instead. We compromised with mid-April. But owing to the change in dates some of the original team dropped out, and there was a monumental foul-up regarding flight tickets as the team member in charge of booking the tickets obtained a refund for himself at the expense of the rest of us. Fortunately, an administrative error on the part of the airline meant that in the end we were able to transfer our tickets to the later dates, and the remaining team breathed easily again.

Finally, air freight was organised and a team of four – Steve Wright, Mike Sharp, Joost van der Valk and me – flew to Bishkek on 12 April. None of us had skied together before. It was Joost's first expedition, but he was an accomplished alpine skier and by far the youngest of us. With a mass of shoulder-length hair, he looked the classic ski bum but was actually a Dutch film-maker. The rest of us were more or less grizzled 50-somethings with distinctly thinning hairlines. Steve had been to Kedar Dome, in India, with Rob Collister in 2000, and Mike had skied mountains in Alaska, South America and Antarctica. By then I'd climbed in Peru and Ecuador, and skied in the Caucasus and Iran. Summitting Denali, in Alaska, had involved both skiing and climbing, and in 2002 I had climbed the 7134m Pik Lenin in the south of Kyrgyzstan.

I slept most of the drive from Bishkek to Barskoon on the southern shore of Lake Issyk-Kuhl, where a homestay had been arranged by our agent. There were cold showers and squat toilets, but the place was clean and tidy and the food good. The other three took up an invitation to take a sauna next door but I had been coughing a lot since the flight and didn't think it would do my chest any good.

Over an early breakfast, the three reported that the owner of the sauna had seemed a little too keen on 'invigorating' birch beatings, which may have been because of how much vodka was consumed. I was glad to have missed the 'fun'. Then we were collected by a *vachtovka*, a 6WD former army truck, for the ascent of the Barskoon Gorge to the Suek Pass at 4100m. The weather was cloudy and damp, so it was no surprise that snowfall began as we gained height, but the road was well maintained and largely clear of snow. We stopped briefly to take a look at the Gagarin memorial stone carved out of a boulder just off the road. Sadly, it had been vandalised by nationalists who had clearly missed the significance of a former foundryman becoming the first human being in space.

Passing the turn-off to the mine at Kumtor, we found that the conditions had deteriorated and snow deepened on the road. We came upon a tracked excavator trying vainly to clear a way through; there had been a metre of snowfall which had avalanched, and the word was that it would take at least two days to clear. Turning back to the Kumtor road, we were advised by locals that it should be possible to cross the Ak Bel Pass, further east, then drop into the Kara Say Valley higher up than our planned access point by road. With no road, it would all be on ski.

So that afternoon the *vachtovka* deposited us by the roadside as near to the pass as possible, to set up camp 1. It was early enough for the other three to carry equipment to a cache about an hour into the ski route, but I didn't feel well enough to join them, so stayed to look after the rest of our gear.

That turned out to be a stroke of luck, as I received a visit from Kumtor's gun-toting security officers who wanted names and passport numbers for their records. They were kind enough to leave a bottle of water with me, but I did wonder whether we'd have returned to find our tents removed if I'd accompanied the rest of the team and no one had been around to speak to them. Their gift meant that I didn't sample the local water supply that resulted in Mike and Steve throwing up for most of the night. Perhaps it hadn't been boiled for long enough. I was still coughing.

Breaking camp, we skied off, kick-gliding without skins, which enabled us to cover more ground on the almost level river flats. I dropped off a waterproof bag with the others at the cache, going on more easily to a campsite 2 over 3 km further. Steve was too unwell to ski back and collect his cache, so when the remaining three of us returned to collect our kit that afternoon we divided his up between us. It was harder work than anticipated, making a double carry on our first day of load-carrying.

Mike and I managed to sort out a decent meal, and my coughing subsided a bit during a stormy night in which Steve reported being sick again. The bad weather continued into the morning, with low cloud and a relentless wind buffeting the tents and keeping us pinned down, chatting and reading. The wind dropped a bit in the afternoon, so Mike and Joost went out for a couple of hours to scout the route to the pass.

That night I was still coughing: hard, sterile, unavailing coughs. Mike and I got on well enough, but neither of us was getting enough sleep. My coughing was disturbing him whilst his snoring seemed to rattle the tent poles, though it might have been the wind. I tried to stifle my coughs in the sleeping bag and Mike told me to just give him a prod and tell him to roll on his side. Both approaches had limited success.

Mike sheepishly confessed, 'On one expedition my tent partner had had enough after a few days and moved in with another pair, but then the whole team came and asked me to move my tent about 50 metres away up the glacier. It was the first time I'd realised there was a problem!'

'Ach, it's not that bad. I'm sure we'll cope, though my coughing doesn't help – it probably makes you more restless.'

Next morning, we all set off with caches in the direction of the Ak Bel Pass, reaching a river, where we hacked through the ice with ice axes to reach water, then continued over more rolling river flats with grass poking through snow on miniature ridges. In some places these were even fringed with mini-cornices. About 8 km out, a metal tripod marked a spot height of 3700m, so we left the caches there, where there was a good chance of finding them again.

On the way back to camp the weather closed in, forcing us to rely on GPS, navigating at times in a complete whiteout. Back at camp, coughing again and mightily tired, I told Steve I was considering my options and might go back to Bishkek or even all the way home, but I also started a course of antibiotics. Hard, compulsive coughing later loosened and I managed to get some sleep.

It snowed all night, pattering or driving against the tent flysheet. When Mike put his head out through the tent zip in the morning, he told me there was a whiteout. I didn't bother to check.

Later that morning there was something of a clearance, so we decided to go and set up camp 3 by the cache tripod. After breaking camp, we set out bearing huge loads, but our spirits were lifted by breaks in the cloud granting glimpses of blue sky, even a hint of sunshine. Beyond the river we came upon fresh snow leopard tracks; cat-like prints as big as my hand, spaced and deep, as though it had headed out across the river flats at a run in the last hour or two. We all scanned the flat lands for any sign of movement but there was none.

As we flogged on in some unaccustomed heat, the mountains cleared of cloud. Mike was stripped down to his white thermal underwear; I could understand the logic of a white base layer, which would reflect the sun's rays, but there was something faintly indecent and distinctly 'grandad' about his appearance. Then his rucksack harness broke, needing an improvised repair. It wasn't our lucky day, as Steve's return spring on one of his Fritschi bindings was lost, but he decided he could manage without it. We camped in a little bowl just below the tripod, even though there was no sign of the small lake marked on the map; there had been hopes that it would provide water and alleviate our inevitable anxiety about using up our fuel supplies to melt snow.

It was time to take stock. At the planning stage the decision had been made to rely on large rucksacks to make double carries and avoid having to ship out sledges, but in the event this was proving to be hard work and time-consuming, especially as we were travelling on breakable

Heading into the mountains

crust with varying depths of unconsolidated hoar crystals beneath. At this rate, transporting all our gear to the planned site of our original first base camp would mean we'd only have a day or two before having to turn back. We were never going to manage the traverse.

What, then, instead? The mountains around us on the western approaches to the Ak-Shirak range were all over 4000m and most looked eminently skiable, so we decided to do some ski mountaineering following a programme that would allow the sick and weary some recovery time on days off when needed.

So the next day Steve stayed in camp, while Mike, Joost and I set out for the highest mountain west of us. I broke trail for 4 km, crossing a big snow basin seamed with shallow gullies and stepped with half-buried scree terraces, to a lunch stop just below a col at 4000m. Cloud hung heavy on the tops, but there was no snowfall – just a cold wind, surprising us with its chill at times as we flogged along in the hazy heat. Mike led on to the crest of the col, where I discovered that

I'd left my camera at the lunch stop – probably the effect of altitude – and had to go back for it.

I followed in their tracks up snow slopes on the right of a broad, rock-studded ridge to a more level section at 4150m. A steeper slope followed, which gradually laid back to the left revealing the summit tripod. It was 3–4 metres tall, built of relatively new timber, with the four legs buttressed by substantial cairns. A small crowning 'cage' at the tip gave us no clue to its purpose. At 4280m on Peak A, as the cloud rolled in and out, we added extra layers of clothing, and Joost attempted to film the scene. The ascent had taken four hours from camp.

The descent was initially a wild sastrugi roller-coaster ride, requiring precise turns if we were not to hook up on one or other of the miniature ice-sculptures, half-buried in recent snow; kind of fun in the sunshine!

Taking a break, Mike commented, 'Well that's a relief!'

'What is?'

'You guys can actually ski! Some tours I've been on have had some right turkeys doing racing snowploughs!'

Mike was pretty stylish himself, with his telemark skis and elegant action.

Below the col, we kept high on long traverses around the big snow bowl, trying to lose as little height as possible before schussing out across the river flats towards the distant camp tripod. That was fine until clouds rolled in again and visibility declined, with a distinct lack of definition in the snowscape – I was suddenly airborne, having skied into an unseen gully, but the soft snow cushioned my impact and with my tracks the others could see enough to make a better job of traversing it. Despite giving the schuss all we'd got, we still needed to kick-glide the last section into camp.

Steve was feeling better and had prospected for water, digging down to find the snow-covered lakelet, so we all filled up and made brews, rehydrating.

The morning brought poor visibility with snow and wind, so Steve, Mike and Joost left at about lunchtime for some low-level exploration of the glacier snouts to the east, but I'd been coughing badly overnight so didn't join them. During the night, temperatures had fallen dramatically and Steve's full Sigg bottle had frozen solid, splitting the metal as the

ice expanded. I dried it out as temperatures rose, and repaired the split with epoxy resin while they were away.

The bad weather continued next day, and it was 2 pm before Steve, Mike and I set out to climb a closer peak to the west of camp. We skinned directly to the steep east ridge, dug a snow pit, and then, encouraged by the snow profile, climbed steadily around exposed rocky outcrops and up steep snow pitches to reach a minor top at around 4000m. Beyond that, a steeper slope led up to the windswept true summit of Peak B at 4207m. It was very clear by then, with fantastic views east into the main range and south towards serried snow peaks on the Chinese border. There was an indicated temperature of -10°C, although with windchill it must have been well below that. Duvet jackets came out as soon as we stopped.

We skied back down the ridge in mixed snow conditions that didn't quite stop us from developing an enjoyable rhythm. Kick-gliding finally took us back to the tents by about 5.30 pm, just as the next wave of snowfall arrived.

Above: Approaching the summit of Peak E
Right: Joost skiing off Peak D

That snow cleared out to leave a cold night and a morning without a cloud in the sky. We were all away earlier, crossing the river basin south-east towards Peak 4557. Passing the waterhole, I noticed it was beginning to smell of silage.

Reaching moraine ridges at the base of the north face of the peak, we decided there could be a risk of avalanche from the face so kept clear by climbing over those ridges to gain the glacier beyond. There we roped up and skinned 3 km of glacier, from 3920m up to 4425m, to a col at its head. There were good views to the south, down into the Kara Say Valley which we should have passed through by then had things worked out according to plan.

Mike, Steve and I attempted the peak to the south-west of the col (D), on foot up a corniced ridge. Steep, deep snow turned Steve and Mike back, but I carried on to reach 4500m, before deciding that trail-breaking in such deep stuff was taking too long to be justified.

Back at the col, Mike and Joost had set off up the 4449m Peak E, which straddled the pass, but Steve and I were content to take a break, topping up on food and drink until they returned. We left the col after 4.15 pm, taking a direct line down the headwall, then cruising along the true right side of the glacier to avoid the hollows and ridges of our ascent up the centre. In 50 minutes of exhilarating skiing, we had reached our roping-up point.

There we discussed whether to climb back over the moraine ridges or take a run following the gorge-like river cuttings through them and continuing under the north face. There was some evidence of avalanche debris, but the face had been stable all day, and a closer look from this angle revealed that the avalanche debris hadn't actually reached the river itself. We went for it; mainly straight-line cruising of the river bends through strikingly wild rock scenery until the angle kicked in and we put in more turns to ski out below the moraine with the whole wide basin lying before us. Only the occasional obligatory photograph interrupted us gliding back to the tents.

Calling at the water hole to fill up, we found it iced over, which lulled Joost into a false sense of security; stepping off his skis he plunged knee-deep into the water beneath the ice. Steve was also caught out, and I only escaped a soaking by flinging myself flat on the snow to one side of the hidden pool. Mike thought it was hilarious, and even the

Regrouping below the eastern moraines

wettest of us could see the funny side. At least we filled our water bottles, however smelly the water – and, to our surprise, we suffered no ill effects from it; even at that height, boiling it for long enough must have been effective.

Another snowy morning kept us tent-bound until 2 pm, when signs of a clearance tempted us to try the 4064m Peak C to the west of the river. Hard snow pellets were sketting, hail-like, out of the roiling clouds, and before long Steve turned back, coughing again. The rest of us continued towards our peak, notable for a bare south-west shoulder of wind-scoured scree. Rounding a blunt snow ridge, we realised that the col ahead was steep, corniced and probably well loaded with new snow. We turned aside to climb the blunt ridge to the right, gaining the highest point of a snow dome, where an icy wind and rushing clouds allowed us only squinting glimpses of snow-capped peaks to the south and west.

In descent, we skied short runs, then a long schuss back to the tents. Just a three-hour outing, but worth it.

It was a warm night with snow from the north loading the flysheets, and then another morning of lighter snow, but with enough cloud to create poor visibility, dampening everyone's spirits.

Joost voiced my misgivings when he said, 'We wouldn't go out in the Alps in these conditions, after the weather we've had. It's warm, and thawing, so the avalanche risk is going to be really high.'

'You're right,' said Steve, 'but we could keep off the mountains while the weather is so poor. Stay low and just travel; have a better look at the area.'

'Well, if we're talking about travelling, then we could go over the pass to have a closer look at the Kara Say approach to the range. We could go light with just a few days' food and fuel; that would make it quick.' Mike had been thinking about the logistics.

'Another possibility,' I said, 'might be to go back towards the road and have a look at that glacial valley further east that comes in from the north and looks like it might run right up to a col east of Kyrgyzia. It would be good to get that climbed if we could.' Kyrgyzia was the only named peak in the range; although the Russian map indicated others that might well be higher, it was probably the highest point visible from the road.

'Yes, said Joost. 'I'd be keen to do that.'

'I'd prefer to go over the pass to check out the Kara Say access, but I'm just not feeling well enough to travel today,' Steve added, coughing a conclusion to his sentence.

'That's you and me decided for tomorrow then,' Mike put in. 'What about you, Joost?'

'Still not sure, but I do feel the need for a change of scene.'

'Yeah, that's tempting,' I said, 'but I can't say I'll have much enthusiasm for skating along river ice if the weather turns out to be good enough to have a go at some mountains. That shouldn't affect anyone else's decision. The tents are both big enough for three at a push, and I can manage on my own for a few days, being very careful when I'm on the hill. I'm undecided, to be honest.' And I was. Very undecided.

We spent the rest of that bad-weather day in the tents, leaving the final decision for each of us to make individually the following morning.

When that morning dawned clear and sunny, I just couldn't give up on the mountains.

I probably wouldn't make the same decision now, but I'd come to feel that this was no hostile environment, or rather that its hostility was in its nature; there was nothing personal about it. I knew all about calculated, vicious hostility in the actions of those seeking to advance their personal interests in the service of a narcissistic psychopath, and not only from the poor guy who subsequently committed suicide as a result of being targeted. This was nothing like that. The odds were not stacked against me. This was fair play, and I was a willing player in a risky game, accepting and managing those risks. In doing so there were discoveries to be made about the environment and about myself, and from those discoveries flowed a sense of well-being. The eminent writer Josephine Hart said, 'Damaged people are dangerous. They know they can survive.' But they can also heal and find themselves at home in a landscape that relates to their 'geography of the soul'.

'You take care, guys, as I will!' And I left them packing while I skinned across the flats to the base of a twisting ridge where a glacial valley came in from the north to meet a ravine cutting through the rocky moraine barrier to the east.

The weather was warm, and the subsidence of snow rafts, triggered by my passage over them, was accompanied by unnerving whumps, although the angle was so shallow that there was no danger of avalanche. The whumps petered out as I gained height on the ridge, keeping to the thinly snow-covered terrain winding around protruding rocks and scree. Only once did I stray left onto a more northerly aspect, where ice under the snow threatened to slide me off into the valley far below.

I skirted the first top on a long traverse to a saddle beyond it, where I snacked at 4000m before winding up around more rock and scree patches to gain the crest of the ridge above. This continued very rocky with precipitous buttresses and steep slopes to the west, but easier-angled snow and scree slopes to the east.

I reached the crest of a snow ridge to find myself perched above the rocky buttresses that I'd seen in profile from lower down, and needing to descend a few metres of knife-edge of snow to reach the flat bay beyond. From there, a steep climb up another snow ridge to where it ran into the rocks of the highest buttress led to a scramble over those rocks. That left just a long plod up the final snow dome to its summit at 4560m.

It looked as though I could extend the climb to another summit by descending to a col and climbing up through ice cliffs, but it was 4 pm, and that would complicate the descent. Besides, I was knackered! A lammergeier passed low overhead on widespread wings, the long tail feathers twitching, the neck craning to scope me out. I took it as an omen. Time to fly.

The ski descent was quite technical, cutting turns around scree patches and avoiding ice lightly covered with snow, but totally absorbing. I was back at the base of the ridge in 45 minutes. More whumps accompanied the run back to the tent which took another hour, as the tracks I had left repeatedly collapsed under my skis; the heat was causing water to melt out of the snowpack, leaving unconsolidated granular crystals, a kind of snow skeleton under the frozen crust, which at that time in the afternoon was of course no longer frozen.

Next morning was also fine, clearing from the north and a little cooler. Heading for the mountain to the north-east, I saw a fox spot me and make a leisurely retreat up the snow slopes, to be lost amongst the shattered rocks above. There was plenty of marmot activity that would explain the fox's interest in the area, and I came across a patch of red-tinged snow next to scattered earth and snow where it had clearly dug a marmot out.

The ridge ahead had looked quite rocky, but steady zigzags up snow ramps found an unexpected continuity that brought me out at a buttress on the ridge, where I took a break. Above, it proved possible to weave between scree patches without straying onto the suspect snow slopes to the south-east, by then in full sun. The angle was good for climbing, and a breeze made the exertion quite comfortable. I gained a shoulder on the ridge, then another with a cairn and marker pole at 4350m. A shadow cut across the snow at my feet, and I looked up to see an eagle pass by, close overhead. Birds of prey seemed to be taking an interest in me. I'd do my best not to become carrion!

From the shoulder, a long, corniced snow ridge rose to a snowy summit. It started easily enough but then narrowed to leave a corridor, no more than two metres wide, between the cornice break-line on the right and ice dropping into the abyss to the left. I did a bit of talking to myself of the 'Buck up and sort yourself out!' variety, before backing up in order to put harscheisen on, continuing precariously to what turned out to be a foresummit. Beyond, a slight drop led to a continuation of the corniced ridge, which became particularly delicate at an oddly-shaped crevasse breach, bridged by an ice block. Then the ridge broadened as another joined it from the left, and I could climb easily to the true summit of Peak F at 4550m. It was the best view so far of Kyrgyzia, standing out above the other mountains to the east and looking very skiable, although the last 100m or so might well have to be done on foot.

I didn't hesitate about keeping the harscheisen biting into the ice until I returned to the foresummit, but there removed them and skied the rest of the narrow ridge with my ice axe in one hand and a ski pole in the other, mostly making short runs ending in left turns against the fall of the slope or side-slipping; very exposed but quite a rush! I took a break at the cairn, and then skied easily on, only troubled by foundering skis in an occasional patch of aerated snow, and still managing to find a good fast runout that took me well across the river flats. The fox was back investigating marmot burrows as I enjoyed the last hour of light and warmth at the tent, reflecting on a brilliant mountain day.

I'd been wondering about seeing how safe the glacier to the east would be, unroped. The angle looked gentle, so major crevasses were probably unlikely – but they could be hidden by a much thinner layer of snow after the rising temperatures of recent days. It was the only objective left, really, so I talked it over with myself and decided it was worth a look. When there is no one else to discuss options with, talking to oneself seems quite reasonable. Otherwise, being alone had made me more alert to my surroundings: sounds, textures, the birds and animals. It confirmed my feeling that this was no hostile environment but one in which I felt relaxed, although when climbing or skiing there was a focused concentration and a meticulous care about the consequences of my actions.

There were no whumps, crossing the river flats, until I entered the valley below the glacier, which was hot, sheltered and south-facing. It was a wild place. A herd of bharal (native 'blue' sheep) watched me, browsing scant new growth on the slopes of yesterday's mountain. The southerly aspect meant that snow was clearing from the face, bringing marmots out of their burrows in numbers. That in turn had aroused

Back at Camp 3

the interest of an eagle that quartered the area on wide wings, in search of the unwary, between periods in which it stood sentinel upon a craggy outcrop above.

There was the dry scoop of a dead glacier on the right above a curiously artificial-looking pile of screes that reminded me of a spoil tip from mining activity in Welsh valleys. Higher up, an ice face bore the remnants of a hanging glacier. It looked as though a series of moraine barriers had created a succession of glacial lakes that were drained when the meltwater broke through, though it was difficult to tell if there was a lake under the ice after the last moraine. If there was, it was a small one. I had lunch just before the last moraine river-gate and tried to dry out boots and socks. The heat was oppressive.

Skinning up the moraine ridge to the left, I emerged onto the glacier at a snow-covered ice shoulder. It was as easy-angled as I'd thought, with no sign of crevasse problems. The way skis distribute one's weight

A thoughtful Joost van der Valk on our way out of the mountains, Kyrgyzia the high peak on his left in the background

over a much larger surface area than a footprint makes them far safer for glacier travel than walking. I skinned on, soaked with sweat, steadily climbing to the head of the glacier at 4155m. There wasn't a breath of wind. The snow dome gleamed in the distance, and I knew I wasn't going to get there in this heat. Dehydration was becoming a serious issue. Time to go down!

I stripped each ski of its skin in turn, resting my free boot on crossed ski poles for balance as I did so in an effort to distribute my weight on that side despite the removal of the ski. I was taking no chances of unknowingly standing over a crevasse. An easy ski down on spring snow turning heavy led through the moraine river gates, with the bharal lifting their heads to watch my passage, out onto the river flats again. A welcome breeze from the north bore a skein of snow geese heading south as I gained the tent and settled in.

The others were due to return next day, so I brewed and read until they turned up, in the early afternoon. They had successfully reached the approaches to the Kara Say Glacier, which looked a perfectly reasonable way to access the range. It was a valuable reconnaissance. There was much sorting of gear and discarding of biodegradable excess food in preparation for packing up next day. Joost moved in with me, and proved to be blessedly free of any tendency to snore.

Next day, massively loaded, we headed downriver, finding more snow leopard prints on the way. Having seen the bharal, I knew what it was hunting. Managing to cross one tributary, we found the next too deep and wide, so we followed it upstream to a bridge where we camped on a grassy platform for the night. Steve's GPS informed us that we were just 1 km from our first camp. The evening light was gorgeous, as were the mountains to the south of us now that we could see them. I think there were some regrets about leaving; Joost leaned over the bridge rail, staring moodily into the swiftly-moving water below.

More snow geese passed overhead early in the morning as we breakfasted before packing up and making the 4 km trek out to meet Alex, the driver, at the road at noon. We actually arrived at 11 but he was waiting already, very excited.

'Welcome! Welcome!' He shook all of our hands.

'Good to see you, Alex.'

'Yes, yes, good to see you too. All of you!'

I think he and the team at the agency had been more anxious than we imagined about our trip.

'You know, this is the first time anyone has done a trip in winter into these mountains. Very good to see you.'

As we drove off in the Toyota, we passed an eagle perched on a boulder right next to the road, huddled under its wings with a fierce glare and a beak like a hatchet.

9

AK-SHIRAK 2006 – FIRST SKI TRAVERSE OF THE RANGE

After the first Kyrgyz ski expedition, I had reached over 5000m before failing to summit on Mt Logan in Canada, and I had soloed Muztagh Ata, at 7546m 'the highest ski peak in the world', in China. In the spring of 2004, I had returned to the Caucasus on ski, then in the autumn of 2005 joined an ill-fated climbing expedition to Szechuan, but during that year had made plans to return to the Ak-Shirak range.

In hopes of avoiding the Suek Pass being blocked with snow, I went in May with an experienced Eagle Ski Club team, including: Mike Sharp, again; Derek Buckle, who had climbed in Tibet, Nepal and Greenland; John Goodwin; and Lizzie Hawker, who had been on the ESC Kalanag expedition in 2003; and finally Alastair Cairns and Anna Seale, who were both doctors with extensive alpine experience as well as having completed serious ski tours in New Zealand and Canada.

This time we were supported by grants from the Mount Everest Foundation, the ESC and the BMC, so costs were kept down, which helped those like Lizzie and me on low incomes. When I'd told Lizzie the cost of the logistics package she'd looked a bit crestfallen and said, 'Sorry but that's too much for me. I paid less than that on Kalanag.'

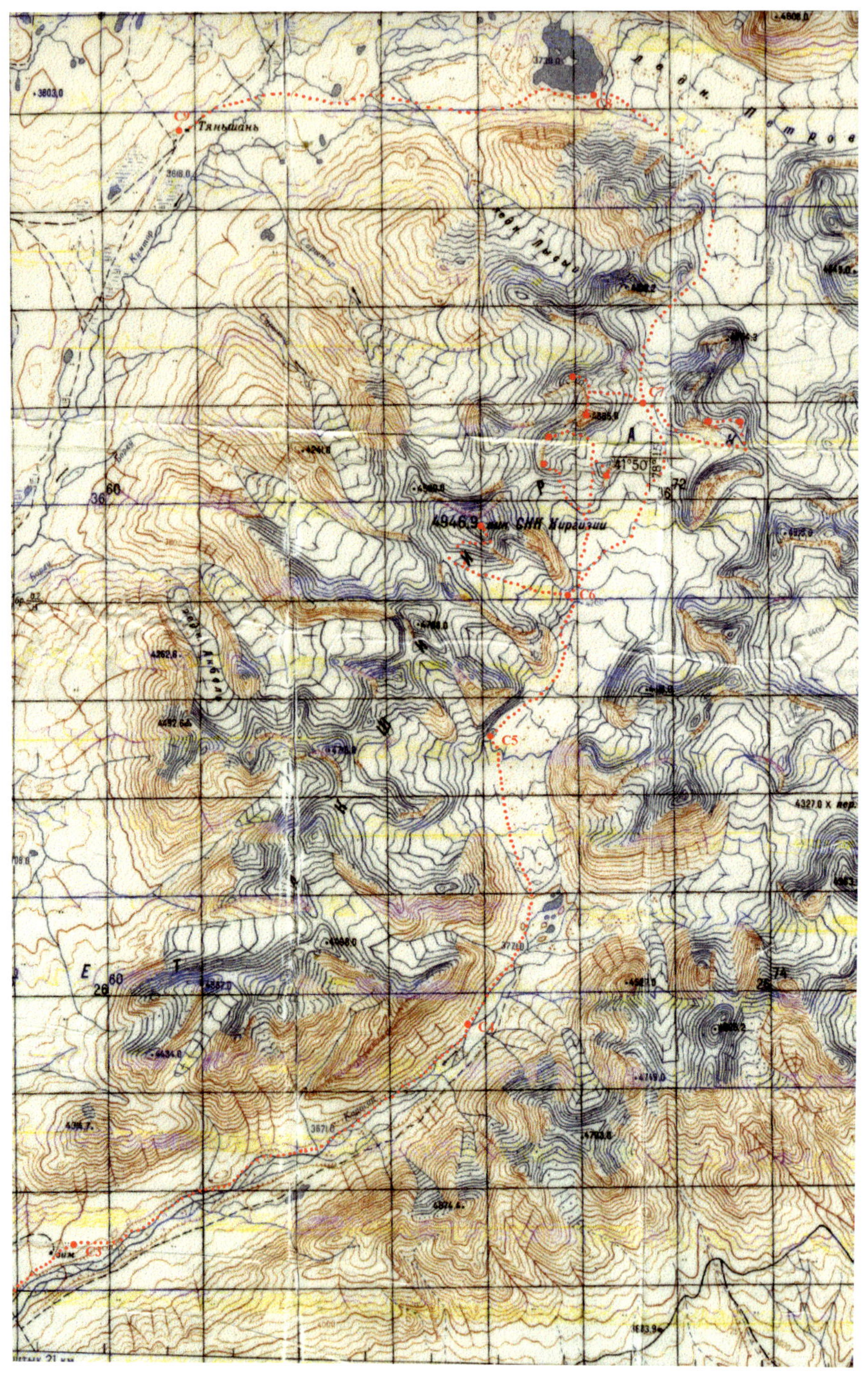

Ak-Shirak route map 2006

'No, no, sorry,' I explained, 'That's not each, but split between the seven of us!' Problem solved.

Flying into Bishkek at 5.10 am on 30 April, we met Rima, our translator and liaison person, and the drivers of our 4×4 truck; not 6WD this time, but we were in no position to argue. Arriving at our accommodation in Tamga, near Barskoon, we found it had been updated and learnt more of the owner's background.

Sergei and his wife, Julia, had both been Soviet Masters of Sport in mountaineering with appropriate support from the state, but that support was withdrawn after independence so they had had to open their home in Tamga as a guest house and were now developing facilities to use it as a base for exploring the surrounding mountains. Sergei confirmed that none of the mountains in the Ak-Shirak range had been climbed as it just hadn't been thought likely to have hard enough routes for climbing interest.

Ski mountaineering didn't seem to have been considered, but I wasn't surprised; the same mindset had applied in British mountaineering, so that British guides had notoriously struggled with the skiing component of their qualification. The house and gardens appeared to be as peaceful as ever, and the walk down to the outside toilet was lined with flowering apple trees, heavy with scented blossom.

I had decided that pulks would enable us to avoid the drudgery of double carries on a trip where we were travelling more than gaining altitude between camps. They were just kiddies' sledges' (standard issue on Denali) suitably adapted by drilling holes and using accessory cord, but attempting more control by utilising plumbing pipework to stabilise towing arrangements and avoid the nasty tendency of pulks without such modifications to wrap their towlines around a skier's legs. We spent the rest of the day assembling pulks and packing rucksacks to leave next morning.

On the drive up the Barskoon Gorge the vehicle struggled on the steep hairpins and there were several stops where the co-driver drew buckets of water from a nearby stream to throw over the engine in time-honoured third-world fashion. The Suek Pass was more or less clear, although there was lots of snow around and an unstable road surface. Rima told us that *suek* means 'white bones', commemorating the deaths of hundreds fleeing famine over the pass during the bad winter of 1916.

As we began the descent it seemed nothing could stop us reaching the Kara Say drop-off point, but the truck became stuck in deep snow at a river crossing near a little settlement. The drivers seemed at a loss and sulked, refusing to countenance suggestions from the team, perhaps because they were put to them by Rima. She apologised for the delay, and eventually a group of local Kyrgyz arrived, placed stones to jack up the truck and loaded more stones under the wheels until it was possible to drive out onto firm ice and across the river. Which was exactly what had been suggested five hours earlier!

The drivers were a lot more careful after that, but more time was lost in the valley below when we needed to show our permit for the border zone at a quite inaccessible army post, tucked away on the far side of the river. It was 9 pm and dark when the truck reached the bridge over the Kara Say River, which marked the point where we needed to turn off up the river valley. The drivers resolutely maintained that there was no road up that valley despite John Turk's report of reaching the glacier by truck that way. After unsuccessfully prospecting for the start of the track in the darkness, I had to accept that the truck was taking us no further. Rima wished us good luck as they left to return to Bishkek while the ski team camped just off the road.

In the morning light I looked out of the tent flap and there were the twin tyre tracks of the rough road up the valley although access from the main road was less obvious; it wasn't exactly a well-travelled route. Unfortunately, that meant another 20 km had just been added to our journey, and all below the snow line. Double carries were back on the agenda.

We hid all the gear we weren't carrying as far away from the road as possible, then set off. The patient and strong, led by Lizzie Hawker, preferred to carry everything on their backs whilst the rest of us lightened our rucksacks by towing lightly laden pulks along one or other of the gravel tyre tracks. Altitude headaches, brought on by our 2000m height gain in 12 hours the previous day, didn't make this any easier. The first day ended at a roaring tributary torrent, uncrossable so late in the day. That meant stashing our kit and walking back for a second load, taking in the background of snow peaks crowding the Chinese border to the south. The night was spent camped on raised grassy islands amongst floodwater rivulets.

Early morning stream crossing on the trek up the Kara Say Valley

By morning, the nightly freeze had reduced meltwater flow to a much more manageable level so each of us was able to cross, barefoot with rolled-up trousers. It was an absolutely perishing triple wade, to carry both loads! Rebooted, we continued following the vehicle track along the river flood plain, dotted with patches of thin snow which never quite became sufficient to justify putting on skis.

Regrouping for lunch at a ruined building, Mike recognised it from 2003. It was evidence of another abandoned Soviet enterprise; Alex, our translator, had mentioned during the previous trip that the foothills and valleys had been extensively grazed before independence. Now the flocks were gone, marmot alarm calls warned of our presence and eagles circled overhead.

Further on, a level shelf in the riverbank looked like an ideal campsite, so we left our kit and went back for second loads. The shelf was above a point where it was possible to access river ice that looked to be neither underwater nor too weak to support the weight of a skier. Hopefully we would make better progress skinning upriver on that ice.

Unfortunately, I discovered that towing pulks over gravel had caused some wear and damage to the plastic runners, so several of us tried to sort out repairs with epoxy resin and sections of bamboo before turning in that night. There was a whispering of snow on the flysheet overnight but I woke, thinking I could hear the sound of animal movements outside the tent. Lying there listening, I realised Alastair was also awake.

'Can you hear anything?' I asked.

'Just the snow.'

'Well maybe it's that, but I thought I heard rustlings like animals.'

He listened more carefully. 'No. Nothing.'

But I was right. In the morning there was a network of rodent tracks around our kit. Luckily nothing had been gnawed. Waterproof containers had the added benefit of sealing any scent in.

The vehicle trail continued more vaguely, but out on the snow-dusted ice it felt good to be on ski and skinning at last, whilst the sledges ran easily over the surface, at least at first. The ice was around a metre thick in places, but elsewhere gravel shoals had reduced its depth to nothing at all. The river could drain through this gravel, so there were stretches where fingers of ice reached into gravel shallows then disappeared.

Most of the gravel banks petered out into more ice within 100m, so we tied skis onto rucksacks, carried them across, and then went back to collect the pulks. It was relatively easy for two of us to carry the pulks in pairs, one of us at the nose and another at the tail of a pair of them. On longer carries the cords cut into our hands so that when there was no continuation ice for a kilometre or so the contents of the pulks would have to be packed into rucksacks in a routine of tedious packing and unpacking; either that or carry the pulks one at a time, sharing the burden on one hand then the other. It was tough going.

At about 4 pm we ran into a wide gravel band and decided to call it a day, camping on a level bank of fine gravel with water nearby. It had begun as a very grey day – 'dreich', as Lizzie put it – but there had been some sunny breaks in the cloud and the mountains seemed to have risen around us as we skinned upriver. The evening was fine, and there was a sense of achievement in having covered about 10 km according to GPS readings.

Our second day on the river began with a long double carry that mercifully didn't feel so bad early in the day. Then it was back to the routine of following ice inlets into gravel banks then carrying loads when further sledging was impossible; all the time drawing nearer to the glacier ahead.

We took the left fork at a junction of glacial valleys, then wound through a succession of terminal moraines that marked the retreat of the glacier. Each of the moraine dams had been broken by outwash rivers, as the lakes that had developed behind them had increased water pressure until a collapse, so that only shallow remnants of moraine lakes lay behind them.

There was no river-gate through the final moraine dam, so we had no choice but to wrestle the pulks up and over it. The far side was a snow slope down onto a much larger frozen lake, so we had a chance to see how our pulks would run. Heavily laden as they were, some obstinately refused to stop rolling whilst others twisted or broke their poles. Patches of isothermic snow collapsing under us would have added

Camping on the frozen river

an almost comic dimension to the chaos if it hadn't been so irritating. Coping with these obstacles, I realised it might become necessary to allow more time to ski out at the end of the traverse.

Once on the lake ice we made good time, although when negotiating semi-frozen linking streams through moraine banks we could see that the ice was often awash with glacial meltwater and it was difficult to judge its thickness. In the lead, I managed to break through, resulting in some impromptu ski wading although the water wasn't deep enough for a serious soaking. I climbed out onto firm ice without shedding my skis and just continued, hoping to dry out on the march.

Cloud was closing in and the glacier snout just 40m away when we decided to camp, high and dry on a gravel bank with meltwater flowing close by. As the tents went up, the first flakes of snow began to fall and continued into the night. All next day snow fell steadily so we took a rest day, filling it with reading, writing and talking, plus a little gear sorting in bright intervals soon curtailed by the next flurries of snow.

Another overcast day began to brighten, but the glacier ahead had looked complex so we decided to carry caches on a scouting mission. Flat light meant that leaders would stumble to a halt on the brink of taking falls off unseen edges of ice and there were several false trails ending at uncrossable crevasses or ice wall blockages. It was a slow business finding a way through. This wasn't an icefall, but it was an extremely convoluted glacier. GPS readings put us higher than expected so we cached our loads at about 4200m, then skied back in improving visibility, which allowed us to straighten out the route, avoiding unnecessary twists and turns and placing wands at waypoints.

Back at the snout of the glacier, a correlation of map and GPS data confirmed that the ice had retreated 2 km since 1972, when the map had last been revised, which meant that spot heights and contours on the glacier were also going to be inaccurate owing to the reduced volume of glacial ice.

'Weird glacier!' Anna exclaimed.

'Oh, yes,' Derek agreed. 'To be honest, I've never seen one like it.'

'Me neither,' Mike added. 'Not in Alaska. Not in Antarctica. It's not as if it's broken up like an icefall with ragged crevasses and tottering seracs, just that maze of ridges and bowls, obviously crevassed but not dramatically.'

Skinning up the Kara Say Glacier

'*Mer de Glace* would describe it, but with bigger waves.'

'No, not really like the sea. I thought it was more like desert sand dunes, but made of snow in this case.'

'It looked less convoluted above the cache, so perhaps it's only a feature at this level on the glaciers. Might be due to the aspect, you know, like penitentes. I just hope the glacier on the way out isn't like that.'

Next morning, our knowledge of the route and good visibility made such a difference to the ascent, reaching the cache by lunchtime. The mountains were spectacular, far more rugged than those Mike and I had explored in 2003. My pulk ran well in the ski track, never overturning, and I was really enjoying being there on the Kara Say Glacier after having dreamed about it for so long.

Lizzie Hawker was in good form, easily arriving at the cache ahead of the rest of us. When I arrived, she was sitting on her pulk looking out over the mountains, very quiet.

'You okay?' I asked, disturbing her reverie.

'Yes. Fine. Just having a quiet moment. It's a wonderful place.'

Although we were to ski together again, climb ice in the Écrins, and walk some of the mountain trails around Chamonix, I would never have thought then that, despite her obvious strength and stamina, this unassuming young woman would go on to become an outstanding ultratrail runner and World 100 km Champion. Hidden depths.

The others arrived and we considered where to camp. Above, outflanking an icefall to the north-west, a sheltered site nestled in the crook of a rocky ridge dropping from Kyrgyzia. We skinned up to check it out, then levelled the snow and pitched our tents. Soon meltwater was boiling for vital brews at our first climbing camp (6).

Strange weather greeted us in the morning, with cloud wreathing the summits, then sinking down to our level, then lifting again. Sudden breaks of sunshine were followed by equally sudden flurries of snow, sometimes blurring into longer showers. We delayed leaving until late morning, and then, as conditions hadn't become any worse or any better, decided to tough it out and explore the glacier bay to the north-east.

Crossing a few crevasses via snow bridges, we emerged onto a glacier plateau with no signs of any further obvious crevasses. Gaining height, the snow dunescape had given way to more conventional glaciated terrain. The weather continued changeable, so to be extra careful we marked GPS waypoints with wands, as our tracks were likely to be blown out or snowed over. Skirting a rock buttress beneath an ice bosse, we skinned up into a snow bowl above it, passing the foot of what seemed to be the south ridge of a peak standing sentinel over a pass to the east of Kyrgyzia; a peak that, in glimpses through the clouds, looked quite skiable.

From the bowl we skinned up the flank of this ridge to the crest where we left our skis, and Derek led the way, on foot, more steeply up the ridge itself. Breaking trail with axe and crampons was heavy going, so he turned it over to me after a while and I reached the icy snow dome of the summit just above rock outcrops. The weather had deteriorated, so there were absolutely no views from the top, but in a summit photo everyone is smiling.

Anna had stayed with the skis, doubtful about the weather, so I climbed quickly but carefully down collapsing snow steps to rejoin her at the ski depot.

'How are you doing?'

'Freezing! Let's just get going!'

We soon skied out below the cloud, following what was left of our tracks aided by the marker wands. Trusting to GPS alone risked magnifying any navigation errors, which was demonstrated on the descent when the GPS was telling me that we had arrived at a waypoint with no wand in sight until the mist rose to reveal it about 50m away. Visibility remained poor, and in flat light we skied through the misty snowscape like a formation snow plough team! When we were arriving at the tents, the weather turned really stormy for us, and it put down 8–10 inches of snow overnight.

It was still snowing at 6 am, so we delayed breakfast until 8; with all the new snow and wind there was going to be a risk of windslab avalanche. Anna and Lizzie were sharing one tent, with Derek and Mike in another while Alastair, John and I made the best of a less prestigious three-person tent that I'd uprated with improved alloy tent poles. With time on our hands we crept into each other's tents to discuss options,

Camp 6 below Kyrgyzia

and I was impressed by how many people could fit, more or less, into a Quasar.

The weather brightened, and by late morning the team decided to skin up onto the glacier above the icefall and scout the route to Kyrgyzia, perhaps getting as far as Kyrgyzia Pass if we were lucky.

A good snow ramp outflanked the icefall above camp, enabling us to gain an undulating but largely crevasse-free glacier above, which we followed, rising steadily to the pass. Roped up with our heads down and buffeted by the wind, we found it hard to keep pace within each rope team, but at least the slope angle never rose to 30 degrees, easing my worries about avalanches. The problem was a bitter wind, tearing the spindrift off surrounding ridges and blowing straight into our faces. That was painful enough for us to keep our heads down, hoods covering as much as possible of our faces. Some resorted to goggles and facemasks of one sort or another, although the bearded contingent enjoyed their natural advantage, such as it was. Occasionally, I would snatch a glance around to make sure we were still on route, but most of the time there was little to see beyond the rhythmic movement of our boots and skis sliding forward in the tracks of the person ahead.

The cold was enough to stop my camera working, and I had to carry it under layers of clothing, hoping my body heat would thaw it out. Punching our ski pole grips into the headwind chilled our fingers to the bone, and high-altitude mitts came out of several rucksacks. At the pass, altimeter readings gave a height of 4600m, and those who hadn't already put on their duvet jackets rapidly did so. By then the camera was working again so I hastily snapped a couple of shots before my fingers froze.

There was a good view of the route onto Kyrgyzia, with feasible options available depending on snow conditions, but so exposed to the wind that an exchange of views, shouted above the windblast, agreed a consensus that there was no way we could continue that day. It felt strange to be standing exactly where I'd imagined the route would go when looking east to Kyrgyzia from a lonely peak in 2003.

Stripping skins in that icy blast meant we needed to bash some life back into our fingers before skiing a relaxed sequence of runs down the glacier with the wind behind us, regrouping at intervals and enjoying the powder. It was so good that Alastair and I skinned back up to try a steeper line between the rocks of the sheltering ridge and an outcropping of ice above the camp. Unfortunately, the surface there had been largely stripped of powder, and proved too crusty for anything resembling a stylish descent.

Overnight, Lizzie recorded a temperature of -18°C inside the girls' tent.

Next day conditions were better. Leaving at 9 am, we headed back up to Kyrgyzia Pass with Lizzie and Anna, Derek and Mike roped together, and my team, including Alastair and John from the third tent, tied in to another rope. There was no telling whether wind-driven snow had obscured any crevasses, so we took no chances as we repeated the ascent of the previous day.

Nearing the pass, we struck off rightwards into a snow bay on the flank of the mountain. The original plan had been to climb up onto the easy-angled west ridge via a notch behind an ice peaklet bearing a chunky cornice, but nearing the peaklet we saw that the climb to the notch looked steep and icy with a large crevasse beneath it waiting to ensnare the unwary. Instead, we took a long traverse line out of the bay to gain the south spur of Kyrgyzia above another ice bosse. There the larger team decided the snow was too unstable to continue skinning, and exchanged their skis for axes and crampons. My team obstinately persuaded ourselves that the spur still looked skinnable – until a warning whump vibrated under my skis, alarming us sufficiently to reach the conclusion that it wasn't.

We kicked steps directly up the spur, warily crossing several crevasses and encountering a variety of snow conditions, to reach the corniced summit ridge. The highest point registered 4954m on my GPS, and I have a photo of Alastair on his knees there, looking as if he is giving thanks to God. It was very clearly the highest peak in this northern half of the range, although peaks to the south appeared to confirm the map's attribution of more than 5000m to a few of them.

During the previous day we had been able to see how the south and east ridges of the mountain defined a precipitous rocky face beneath the summit, and there were huge cornices hanging over that face from the ridge on which we now stood, keeping well back from any cornice break-line. In descent, the ridge reinforced our impressions of those cornices to the left, whilst the convex slope we had climbed dropped out of sight to the right. It was an intimidating position, and no surprise that Anna had some anxiety leading the way down our snow steps, but with a moment or two to catch her breath and some reassuring words from Mike, who was belaying her, she was on her way again.

We all descended very carefully to the ski depot, then one by one skied slowly and exactly down the track of our ascending traverse

Alastair on the summit of Kyrgyzia

back into the snow bowl; snow conditions were simply not safe enough for any other strategy. From the bowl we could relish the wonderful glacier skiing back down to camp, although some lovely spring snow sometimes surprised us with outcroppings of crud.

At camp, Alastair's celebratory drams of whisky went straight to our heads via empty stomachs too used to short rations by then. Our elated laughter complemented those moments of stillness we had all experienced in this empty snowscape. There was something hugely satisfying about being the only people in these mountains, climbing peaks no one had climbed before, skiing slopes no one had skied before in magnificent alpine scenery with acres of other unclimbed peaks to choose from. One could imagine what it must have been like for the early pioneers in the Alps.

Next day we woke to a morning of tiny snow crystals precipitating out of high thin clouds wafting around the peaks. Familiar territory to the north-east appealed in those conditions, so we headed up the glacier more or less on the same track followed when climbing what had since been named Sentinel Peak. This time with the intention of climbing the next peak in the chain.

Mike skiing off Kyrgyzia

Reaching the snow bowl below Sentinel Peak, we skinned steeply up a snow face to the right of a rock rognon to gain a broad ridge, almost a glacier shelf, that rose towards our chosen peak until it ran into a steep face overhung with cornices. We skinned a line below that face to take us to the col at the foot of the ridge from which the cornices projected. The north face of our mountain was very steep and rocky, so that corniced east ridge, almost a narrow face, was our only option for an ascent.

Most of the team left their skis at the col, but I managed to skin up, using harscheisen, to within 100m of the summit, where the ridge became too narrow to allow any further zigzags and too steep to climb direct on ski. Derek, Lizzie, Anna and Mike passed me on foot while I stashed my skis and sorted out crampons before following them. After 50m Derek stopped, as the exposure was beginning to tell on the team. The steep drops on either side were quite intimidating as the ridge narrowed, and Anna and Mike were not inclined to continue to the summit. I soloed past to the summit proper, jabbing my ice axe repeatedly into the snow to make sure there was still ice beneath and I wasn't on the cornice break-line. The GPS read 4831m – higher than Mont Blanc again! There were good views of Kyrgyzia as the ravens that had shadowed us from the glacier shelf now flew curiously past, croaking.

Derek unroped and came up to join me for a couple of photos: 'Raven Peak would be a good name for this one.'

'Good idea,' I said.

Then he and I reversed our ascent to where Mike was belaying Anna down to safer ground. The rest of the team made their own minds up about whether or not to attempt the exposed summit. John and Lizzie were the last ones down.

At the col a sharp arête rose very steeply to twin peaks to the east, but was too serious for us to attempt in the time we had left that day. Instead, after a lunch break, we skied easily down the broad ridge until tempted by a handsome minor summit where it terminated to the east. On foot, a very awkward bergschrund required a knee brace in the crevasse to crampon into steep ice above. That ice gave way to an easier snow-ice slope and a compact rocky summit at 4658m, all climbed in crampons and named Point Anna after Anna.

Cautious skiing around the icy bosse regained the line of our ascent, and then, one by one, each of us skied down the steep snow face into the bowl, regrouping before heading back down the glacier. It was fine skiing on good snow, and Alastair easily won the race that he initiated to collect the most marker wands left from our earlier trip.

A cloudy night with a little snow faded to an uninspiring grey morning in which we examined our options during a huddled conference, shifting from foot to foot in the cold snow.

'Weather could go either way,' I said, 'so I don't fancy anything ambitious.'

'No, and I don't like the idea of crossing that chaotic glacier to get at the peaks on the other side,' Derek added.

'There's not a lot left to do from here then, really,' Anna pointed out with devastating logic.

'True,' Mike acknowledged, 'but we could go up and camp on the watershed; the high pass at the head of the Kara Say Glacier. From there we could come back this way if we saw anything interesting on the way up, or see what we can do around or over the pass.'

'There are some peaks either side of the pass that could be interesting, looking at the map,' I added.

'And we would get a better idea of the descent from the pass to the Petrov Glacier in case it's as tricky as the Kara Say.' We were already thinking about how to organise the days we had left.

'That would be useful,' Alastair agreed. 'I don't want to get stuck in the mountains and let down my colleagues at work.'

Working in his local hospital meant Alastair tried to avoid crisis management, although to judge from some of his stories, not always as successfully as he would like.

'Okay, shall we pack up and move on? Are we all agreed?' I put the question, and there were nods all round.

Alastair immediately dragged his empty sledge upslope to see how it would run, and found it lively enough to almost take out one of the tents as he swept down, barely in control. It was welcome comic relief as we left a camp where we had come to feel quite at home after our long trek into the range.

We towed the pulks out of camp mid-morning, keeping as high as we could on the left of the glacier, winding up through the crevasses. Mike's team of four led on one rope whilst my tent-team of three followed exactly in their tracks, unroped. It was a variation on a tactic I'd seen used by Sherpas in Nepal.

The weather cleared by lunchtime with no wind at all, so the heat on the glacier was intense in the sunshine. We took several stops to drink, snack and cool down. Owing to the heat there was little appetite for more than putting up the tents on gaining the broad level pass, but nobody did so until I'd checked out the descent glacier. It looked straightforward enough on skier's left, and the stunning prospect of the eastern half of the range which opened up before us from the pass inspired the name of Prospect Pass. At 4500m, it was a wide-open saddle with little shelter available, and the likelihood of hidden crevasses. Mike and I probed the area carefully with the same thin alloy poles that would have been used to locate a skier buried in an avalanche. Others marked the perimeter of the probed area with wands, so that we knew where it was safe to walk around unroped, before pitching the tents. Digging out a latrine with a snow-block wall for shelter and privacy was a priority. Then it was time for some serious rehydration, enjoying the evening sunshine that stayed with us longer at this altitude.

We woke at 6.30 am to a morning with not a cloud in the sky. Leaving camp at around 9 am, we found the morning chill was quickly dispelled with the effort of climbing up into the glacier basin to the north-west of the pass. To the left, the broken east face of Peak 4865.9m was frozen in the act of tumbling seracs in slow motion into the bay below, whilst the north-east ridge, to its right, rose leftwards from a col to the corniced summit. To the right of the col, another ridge rose in rocky steps and ice bowls to the final peak, over 4800m in this chain.

We skinned steadily up to the col and decided to climb the left-hand, higher peak first. Anna stayed at the col but the rest of us climbed on good névé, in two ropes of three, up the ridge. Derek led, sorting out a good line that outflanked crevasses, cutting into the ridge on the left, by taking to ice slopes on the right until finally gaining the summit at an indicated 4876m. We kept well back from the corniced edge, but that meant accepting the exposure of the narrowing final section of ridge, which generated a few nervous comments.

The views west towards Kyrgyzia and Raven Peak were particularly fine, but we could now clearly see the route of some curious tracks encountered on the ascent. They seemed to have been made by a hare that had come up the ridge from the direction of Raven Peak, descending the ridge we had just climbed but not quite crossing the very summit.

'A *hare?*' Anna was surprised when we told her about it, lunching back at the col. 'Well, that's got to be the name for this peak, then.'

After lunch, I led off right of the col, up the south-facing ridge of the slightly lower peak. The snow was not in good condition by then, alternating between rotten mush over ice, riven with trickles of water, and soft heavy snow which slid underfoot or balled on crampons. It was hard to hit a rhythm with such clumsy climbing. There were scatterings of feathers in places, indicating predation by some sort of raptor in the absence of any tracks, and we'd seen an eagle circling on widespread wings earlier. That contributed to our decision to name the mountain Eagles Peak, although it was also an opportunity to celebrate the Eagle Ski Club.

Anna had roped up with Mike, so we all made it to this summit via a final narrow ridge. Far below lay the enormous scar of Kumtor opencast

Derek approaching the summit of Pik Karga, with Pik Koyon and Eagles Peak in the background

gold mine, where an occasional faint boom of blasting was accompanied by a puff of yellow smoke. It was a reminder of another world.

Returning to the col, we filled our water bottles from a melt pool in the ice just below, then lazed in the sunshine, finishing leftover snacks, before skiing good spring snow back to our camp.

The weather at 6 the following morning was totally overcast, and I wondered about making a run for it down the exit glacier, but by 7 am heavy snowfall left us with little option but to sit it out. Soon after 8 am, sunny intervals were intruding between snow showers, offering some hope for an exploration of the glacier east of the pass, but first I led a scouting party to check out the exit route more thoroughly. We skied down far enough to be reassured, then skinned back up to camp, wanding the route despite improving weather. Then the whole team set out for the eastern glacier bay. This was bordered to the north by a long, mixed ridge that we had begun to refer to as the Portjengrat, because of its resemblance to that Swiss ridge in the Alps. To the south lay the bulk of a peak that we had named Peak Divide, because it divided this glacier bay from another to the south-east.

Resisting the temptation to attempt routes on either the Portjengrat or Peak Divide, we pushed on to gain what we saw as a pass at the head of the glacier, only to find that it was no such thing; on its far side there was no passage down the steep, unskiable rock and snow slopes that fell abruptly into a big glacier bowl below. The arm of the glacier to the south-east that we could have accessed from lower down the Kara Say ended similarly, in a precipitous drop-off into the same glacial bowl. There was a possibility of outflanking those drops by skiing steep slopes off Peak Divide, but they were far too steep to ski with pulks, so there was no way out in this direction. We would be compelled to exit by the escape route scouted that morning. Any exploration of the peaks surrounding the glacier bay below us at this point would have to be accessed from the Petrov Glacier well to the north-east of us.

Cloud gathered and snow showers began to blow in as we took a break for lunch but there was sufficient confidence in retracing our tracks that we skinned up the most easterly peak of the Portjengrat, which turned out to be the only peak on the whole trip that we managed to ascend on ski all the way to the summit.

As we were congratulating ourselves, Derek piped up; 'I think that rocky point over there is actually higher.'

'No way. This is the summit!' Alastair replied.

'Seems that way to me,' Anna agreed.

'Hmmm … I'm not sure about that, and we've got time to check,' and with that Derek set off along the mixed linking ridge.

Dave's variation descent of Pik Karga

I took a GPS reading of 4720m, then followed the others trailing after Derek with varying degrees of enthusiasm. The snow was a bit soft, but to my surprise the rock was granite, reminiscent of Chamonix granite on routes like the Forbes Arête. It made for very enjoyable scrambling to a summit like a kind of turret with slanting pinnacles like twin cannons pointing at the sky. The team took it in turns to chimney up between the cannons to a constricted high point that ironically also registered 4720m. Returning along the ridge to the snow summit, Derek and Alastair became involved in a bantering wrangle about which summit was the highest, snow or cannons. I made a mental note to diplomatically name the peak Snow Cannon, allocating it twin summits.

We skied down, then cruised back to the point at which we had entered this glacier bay. There was constant light snowfall, but sufficient visibility not to have to worry about navigation, skinning back up to the campsite. John fell behind for some reason, and we all waited for a while without any signs of him making much progress. Some members of the team were getting cold, so I sent everyone else on to get settled into camp, unpacked my duvet jacket and waited for John, alone at a point where I could see him and the others, at least until they disappeared over the brow of the glacier. There was no sense in all of us getting cold.

When John did arrive, I asked, 'Are you okay?'

'Yes, fine, just thought I'd take a bit of a break. I hadn't realised anyone was waiting for me.'

'Well, it is snowing, and this is a glacier, with crevasses, and it is mid-afternoon. It may seem benign enough but if you'd gone into a crevasse and no one knew, it could have been a long time before anyone found you. Not a good idea to be travelling on your own. No harm done, but let's try to stick to what's left of the tracks and stay sufficiently apart so that we don't both fall in if a crevasse does open up under one of us. I've got a rope but let's hope we don't have to use it.'

'Oh, sorry; hadn't really thought there was anything to worry about,' and he set off while I packed away my jacket before skinning after him back to camp. Spending such an extended time in the mountains could tend to encourage a false sense of security, but on the other hand it was no surprise that each of us would have our own quiet moments amongst such wonderful scenery.

Lizzie Hawker at the col between Pik Koyon and Eagles Peak, with Pik Karga in the background

On our final day on the glaciers, snow showers were continuing at first light but diminished through the course of the morning as we packed up. As we left Prospect Pass, bearing left for the first marker wand, somehow the slope felt steeper than it had on reconnaissance. We coped by making wide, sweeping snowplough turns that slowed the pulks and kept them on a more even keel. Perhaps I had been lucky to find the 'sweet spot' in the distribution of weight between my rucksack and pulk, since my pulk behaved impeccably and was soon down onto easier slopes. Others had more mixed fortunes, with Mike's pulk rolling repeatedly, but we all managed the initial slope without any serious mishaps. By that time most of the plastic waste plumbing pipes that we had built into the haul systems to give them more rigidity had cracked and broken, rendered brittle by the low temperatures. Throughout the trip, all of us had at one time or another attempted repairs using duct tape with varying success; some had been reduced to simply towing with climbing accessory cord. Whatever the state of the towing rigs, there was no doubt that controlling the pulks had become more difficult despite the lightening of loads as food and fuel was consumed.

When the slope eased, we skied straight down the glacier, letting the skis run or snowploughing according to taste, and regrouping at intervals. As we were gliding through spectacularly beautiful mountain scenery, our speed was probably more than first impressions suggested; a crevasse suddenly appeared ahead of me, requiring a smart left turn to avoid it. As the angle of the glacier declined there was some kick-gliding to maintain momentum, but when I encountered some isothermic collapsing snow, I began to worry about crevasse danger, so a leading group of four was roped up to break trail as before. More isothermic snow created more anxiety in the lead team, so we took a break for lunch on a moraine mound and relaxed, eating and chatting in the sunshine.

I had already noted the monolithic cliffs flanking the steep glacier that fell from the peak looming over the junction of the glaciers. They were about 300m high and just off vertical, cracked but not stepped, and would probably offer good rock-climbing. Then it clicked: like Snow Cannon's ridge, they would be granite. Whereas to the west of the range the rock had been mostly rotten metamorphic schists, nearing the centre granite was now the norm – and that also made sense of the gold mine. Gold deposits are often associated with granite batholiths; the masses of igneous rock mineralise veins within the surrounding rocks owing to their enormous heat. I love it when a landscape makes sense!

After lunch, I led off down the glacier with the skis skittering on snow-crust and ice nearing the snout. Knowing how quickly things can go wrong on ice, I stopped, leaving my load and skis to check out the snout in crampons while the others waited. Hard blunt ice, running with meltwater, dropped suddenly about four metres to more ice and gravel bordering an outwash stream. We weren't going to be able to ski that.

Returning, I briefed the team. 'Right, we need to put crampons on, and axes might be useful on the steep bit; carry skis and rucksacks, then come back for the pulks. I'll set up an ice screw, which we can lower them from. So we'll need to organise people to receive the pulks below and relay them across the stream to a safe spot out of the way while the next one is being lowered. If you don't like the idea of climbing down the ice with your rucksack, then pass it down to someone below.'

As the rest of the team went to sort out their kit, Mike sauntered over, looking quizzical. 'You reckon we need crampons on this? Doesn't seem too bad.'

'It gets worse, trust me …' I said.

Despite sounding complicated, the scheme worked well, with individuals using their initiative and the team operating like a well-oiled machine. After lowering the last pulk, I retrieved my ice screw and climbed down to join the others.

Mike came over, smiling broadly; 'Phew! I was bloody glad to have crampons on, on that. Deceptive!'

'Told ya!' And we both laughed.

With skis on rucksacks, we dragged the pulks over ice flats and moraine outwash, following the stream down to a gravel beach on the shores of Lake Petrov. The next section along the lakeshore looked difficult. The lake ice didn't inspire confidence, even if we could get over the selvedge of water that separated it from our shore. The beach petered out into a jumble of rock between us and the service road that arrived at the pumping station on the other side of the lake.

We discussed whether to push on or not but after travelling 10 km, we agreed to camp on the beach and make our way to the old weather station next day for a pick-up the day after. That was a day earlier than the agent had arranged, so I used the satellite phone to rearrange the collection time.

It was warmer camping on the fine gravel of the beach; a remarkable location, with 5–10m ice cliffs at the glacier snout frozen by the cold of winter in the act of calving mini-icebergs into the lake, and with a backdrop of towering snow-clad mountains. Across the lake's expanse of ice, the lights of the pumping station twinkled like the stars that were emerging in the night sky as darkness fell.

Breaking camp next day, we dragged the pulks along the gravel shore to where it gave out into 35-degree slopes of moraine and avalanche rubble falling into the lake from the flank of the mountain. Patches of snow lodged amongst the increasingly chaotic rockery, and again the team worked well together, managing the pulks through this obstacle course. Towing, carrying, hauling by the central linking strut between pulk poles according to need, we made steady progress, but it was a nightmarish business. After 2 km of that, we reached the pumping station where the Kyrgyz guys in residence made us all strong sweet tea. It was much appreciated.

Then we moved on, towing the pulks along gravel roads, looking for a way out. Towing was proving increasingly difficult as the runners of the pulks were now worn through in places after the harsh treatment on the trek in. Holes had appeared and these were now scooping up stones that collected in the base of the pulks, adding to their weight as we toiled on.

Then Mike was picked up by a passing spoil truck, but there was no room for anyone else. Watching the truck disappear around a bend, I wondered if that would be the last we would ever see of him. The workings had become much more extensive than in 2003 with a network of bulldozed roads that was becoming a navigational challenge. It looked as though they might be planning to dam the whole valley!

Uncomfortably, we took a break for lunch amongst the wasteland of mine-workings, disturbed by its ugliness. Just afterwards, Mike turned up with a mine security pick-up and a minibus. He had persuaded the authorities to ferry us to the abandoned meteorological station for our rendezvous. It meant we would be off their land and no longer a potential security threat or a problem for passing trucks, so I could

Camp 8 on the lakeshore at the snout of the Petrov Glacier

understand their co-operation – but it was more generous than that. Perhaps because of our wasted appearance, they left us with a cardboard box full of sandwiches and rolls. It was the first bread we had tasted in 17 days, but the delight of the vegetarians turned to disappointment when all of the rolls turned out to have meat fillings.

It shouldn't have been a surprise; a culture which has herded animals for thousands of years has difficulty coming to terms with vegetarianism. That caused a bit of an incident when we went out for a meal back in Bishkek: one of our vegetarians completely lost it on finding meat in the dish he had ordered. The language problem didn't help, but it was clear that the poor waitress on the receiving end of his tirade had no idea what the problem was and just thought he was crazy.

We camped at the rear of the abandoned met station, and I had time to reflect that the distance seemed much further than I'd expected from the map. Without the lift from Security, we might not have made it. Perhaps I was just used to the speed of skiing.

'The head of security was quite relaxed about our presence,' Mike filled me in, later. 'They even run tourist trips in the summer.'

'That's a bit different from the armed reception I had in 2003 while you guys were out of camp.' I laughed. 'Perhaps it's a PR exercise. I think they've had some claims from locals who have got ill since the cyanide spill into the water supply back in '98. When Barskoon had to be evacuated.'

'Could be. Makes sense.'

John was up and out at 6 am for some bird-watching, although as we weren't expecting the pick-up until 12 noon, the rest of us made a more leisurely start. That rapidly became a scramble to pack up when the truck arrived at 9.30, but we were soon on the road. Stopping for a comfort break at the top of the hairpins in the gorge, we saw a lammergeier flying low over our heads, and we couldn't help noticing the potential of the surrounding area for further ski mountaineering. Back at Barskoon, all the orchards were full of blossom and the crazier of us of us went swimming in Lake Issyk-Kuhl. It was icy cold!

In Bishkek, by contrast, temperatures were in the 30s and we all welcomed our hotel's swimming pool. It was another world, but a hankering for the mountains took us out of Bishkek on our remaining contingency day to visit the Ala Archa region of the Kyrgyz Range, just a few hours' drive from the city, walking in the alpine meadows and spotting ibex.

Rima was a great help, as we had decided to translate our name suggestions for the peaks we had climbed into Kyrgyz or Russian, more in keeping with our host country. Sentinel became Pik Chasovoi, Raven became Pik Karga, and Hare, Pik Koyon. Point Anna and Eagles Peak we retained to reference our presence, and Snow Cannon didn't seem to have a suitable translation. With Kyrgyzia that made seven first ascents, and Rima promised to pass on the details of their names and exact locations to be added to the records of the Kyrgyz Alpine Club.

Rima was not going to remain in the country for much longer, though. She belonged to the Dungan minority of Chinese Muslims. Known as the Hui in Xinjiang, many of them had fled to Kyrgyzstan, then part of the Russian Empire, during the Dungan rebellions in the 19th century. Since Kyrgyz independence, the Dungan had suffered discrimination, one of the unfortunate consequences of the formation of nationalist governments in former Soviet republics. So Rima, barred from qualifying as a teacher, was planning to emigrate to China and settle within the Dungan community in Xinjiang.

It was another reminder of a very different and rapidly changing world, but one in which the facts were no easier to pin down here than in the UK. Rima insisted that the statue of Lenin that dominated the square outside the Kyrgyz parliament had been moved to a less prominent position in the city when the country became independent in 1991. She simply believed that we must have been mistaken when Mike and I assured her that I'd had my photo taken next to the statue in parliament square just three years earlier in 2003. Recent research indicates that the statue was taken down later that year and re-erected in front of the National Museum behind Ala-too Square. Perhaps it was a sign of the respect still shown to Lenin; demotion rather than destruction. On the other hand, it may have been an assertion of independence, since Rima maintained that it faced a building housing an American organisation; who knows? Bishkek has both US and Russian military bases at the nearby airport.

As I write about the Kyrgyz approach to the statue it reminds me of how endless prevarication in Bristol finally resulted in the tearing down of the Colston statue during a Black Lives Matter demonstration. Kyrgyzstan at least deserves credit for achieving a less acrimonious outcome.

10

AK-SHIRAK 2007 – EXPLORING NORTH OF THE PETROV GLACIER

2007 was the 150th anniversary of the founding of the Alpine Club, and a number of celebratory events were organised for the occasion. I offered to run another expedition to the Ak-Shirak range on ski in early April, which would mean that at least one event could effectively begin before the main European Alpine season. Our views north of the Petrov Glacier in 2006 had revealed that there were some fine mountains to ski, and the map suggested a route to explore the glacier bays of the north-east of the range.

A team of five signed up. Stuart Gallagher and Gordon Nuttall had been with me on Mount Logan in 2003. Stuart had a background of expeditions to Central Asia and South America, whilst Gordon had made some extreme descents in the Alps and been on the Cumbrian Everest expedition, in 1984. Gethin Howells and Adele Long had climbed Kilimanjaro and made extended ski tours in the Wapta Icefields in Canada; I had skied with both of them in France and the Pyrenees. Adele was my partner at that time, and in addition to being Alpine Club members, we were all Eagles.

In Bishkek things did not go smoothly. Our pulks were all packed in one bag, but it did not arrive with the other baggage, so that forced

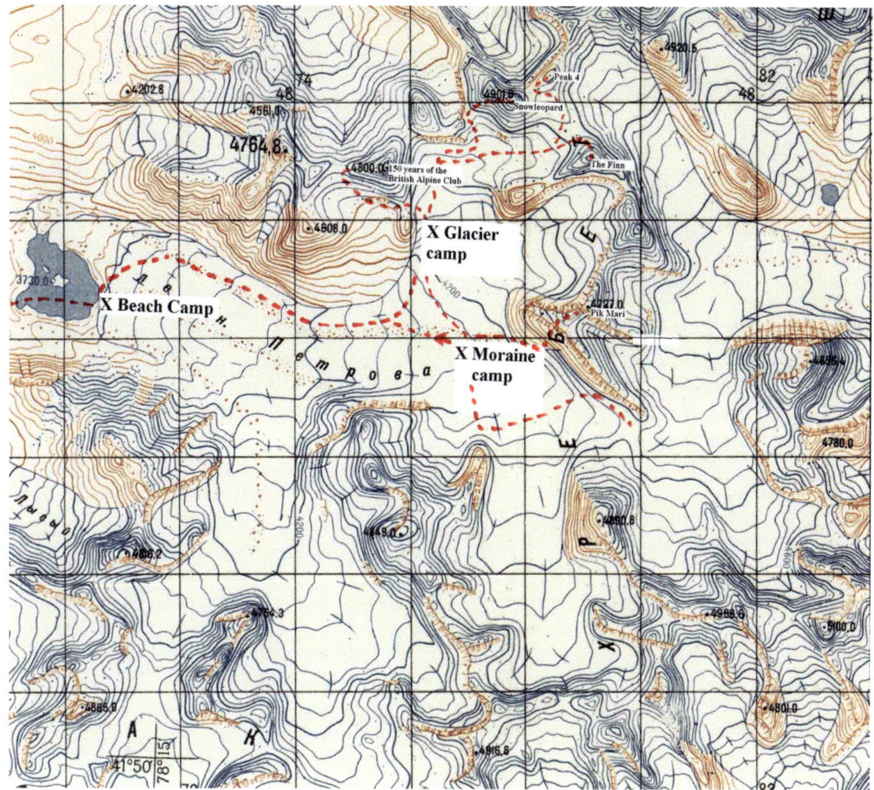

Ak-Shirak 2007 route map

us to spend a day waiting for the bag to arrive in the city. Fortunately, extra accommodation costs were covered by compensation from Aeroflot. Then, after driving to Tamga, near Barskoon, Gordon discovered he had left the inner tent that he'd been using as a pillow back at the hotel in Bishkek. A phone call to ITMC, our agents, meant they could collect it from the hotel and send it by taxi overnight to Tamga, but it cost another $120. It was not a good start to the trip.

At Tamga, our host Sergei had taken over the house next door and was fitting it out as a hostel to cater for the trekking groups that visited in summer. There was double glazing, an inside toilet and showers – but no hot water, as the tank was too low to deliver any pressure to the taps; and the beds were shivery cold so early in the year.

On the drive up the Barskoon Gorge we passed children who rode as if they had been born in the saddle herding sheep and goats, cattle and horses towards higher pastures. The streams of animals parted as we inched our way through. Approaching Kumtor Mine, I realised that not only the road but also most of the slopes below 3800m were clear of snow; quite a contrast to 2003 when a 6WD vehicle had been abandoned after straying off the road into deep snow.

Dave, who was in charge of Kumtor security, turned out to be a former British police officer with a background that included a familiarity with firearms. A routine search of our vehicle revealed that Igor, our driver, had a pistol in the glovebox. Dave's deputy wanted to confiscate it before we entered the site, but Dave had been talking to us while the search was going on and was convinced that we didn't pose a security threat. The armed security team escorted our vehicle to the pumping station.

'There's a pack of about 16 wolves on the site,' Dave told us as we unloaded. 'They're thriving because mine security keeps the hunters out – but watch out for your food supplies. They scavenge a lot, and associate people with food.'

'And they won't be scared of us, I suppose,' I queried.

'Not as scared as those that are hunted but still wary. You should be, too. And if you get into trouble, you can call on us for help. We've got a rescue team, just in case. Not like you'd find in North Wales, but they could help and there's a clinic at the mine.'

'Thanks, much appreciated. We don't have a doctor on the team this time, although a couple of us are qualified first aiders who have been trained for more remote areas.'

'Worth having, but let's hope you don't need their skills. Good luck!' And the security team escorted Igor back to the site gates.

Despite the lack of snow, Lake Petrov was solid ice, so we sorted out the pulks and packed our kit for transit. This year our pulk haulage system had been updated using much more durable plastic pipework designed to withstand water pressure and connected by compression joints, which made assembly far easier. Just before we set off, Dave arrived with the wands we had left in the truck; altitude forgetfulness or jetlag, I guess.

Skinning easily across the lake in only 40 minutes made a mockery of our herculean efforts to traverse the rocky shore in 2006. Despite the lack of snow at the road, temperatures were cold enough to keep the lake ice frozen right up to the shore. Pitching camp on the gritty beach below the glacier snout, all of us were suffering from altitude headaches and dizziness, resulting from the 2000m height gain during the five-hour drive.

At about 5 pm, I was surprised to see two skiers skinning across the ice towards us. They chose a site about 70m away from us, and I let them get their tent up before sauntering over for a word. They were Joris and Wytze from the Netherlands, who had read my Mount Everest Foundation report on our 2006 expedition, and decided they'd like to visit Ak-Shirak too. There was a certain tension in the conversation, and I could tell that neither party was looking forward to competition.

'We are going to go up to where you had a camp on the pass last year. Prospect Pass, is it?'

'Yes, up that right-hand glacier.'

'There look like some interesting mountains around there. Then we come back here and will try to work out a route back down valleys through the range to the north to one of the Issyk-Kuhl villages. And you?'

'We're going north-east, to the left, to have a look at those mountains and follow a loop over one pass to a further glacier, then back onto the Petrov Glacier via another pass.'

'Not likely to see each other after today, then.'

'Perhaps not.' I think we were both relieved. 'Interesting pulk you have.'

'Yes, we take turns with it, travel light.' He could see I was puzzled by the oval of bright blue plastic like a big shallow bucket. 'It's a baby bath. We bought it in Karakol. I think it will do the job.'

'Let's hope so!' But I retained some doubts.

The Dutch had skied in some interesting places, Mongolia for example, and claimed to have made some first ascents, but told me they never completed any reports, just left a cairn to disappoint any subsequent climbers. It seemed a strange approach to me. We swopped email addresses before I left, but I never heard back from them after emailing to query what they had done on my return to the UK. I never heard how they got on with the baby bath either.

They were off early the following morning while we were still packing up our caches to take up to around 4000m on the Petrov Glacier, where it branched to the left. Taking the glacier direct delivered us into a maze of crevasses and ice canyons. Some of the steep descents

Crossing Lake Petrov below the ice cliffs

into those canyons were really unsuitable for pulks, so I suggested we tried a return route further to the south, crossing the glacier to see if the line the Dutch guys had taken would be better.

This would have been near our descent route in 2006, but having agreed the strategy, I was delayed taking GPS readings to waypoint the cache, and by the time I had followed the others across the glacier they had plunged back into the convoluted centre again. I didn't follow, but carried on with the alternative route alone, arriving in camp ahead of the rest of the team, having enjoyed much more open skiing. None of us was very gracious about the mix-up, our grumpiness in part attributable to persisting altitude headaches.

Steady snowfall greeted us in the morning, and Adele, Gordon and I were still complaining of altitude headaches. We agreed a rest day. By 1.30 pm the snow had eased somewhat, Gordon was feeling better and Gethin was feeling bored. They came to ask me if I was interested in prospecting a route up the glacier to the left. Stuart and Adele weren't tempted, but I finished up lunch and followed them.

Skinning up the Petrov Glacier

As we climbed it was clear that the main medial moraine stretched in a rock and dirt stripe all the way from Lake Petrov up to the Dark Tower, itself a big outcrop of moraine and ice, probably resulting from pressure at the junction of the main glacier with a tributary to the north. We crossed the moraine on foot just below the tower, then skied down the slopes feeding into the main ice canyon back to the lakeshore. Or nearly so. Skiing a gentle scoop towards the lake, Gordon, in the lead, came to an abrupt halt. Instead of gently joining the lake ice, the scoop ended in an ice cliff about 5 metres high, with Gordon perched on the brink. I suggested we stepped up the side-slope to the right in search of a less damaging descent – and, sure enough, the slope beyond followed the edge of the ice, descending steadily to a boulder beach, where an easy step down put us onto the frozen lake.

Not entirely trusting the ice, we roped up and headed for an ice headland that was enclosing this bay on the left, keeping a respectful distance from the ice cliffs that, judging from the debris, must have collapsed periodically onto the lake ice. The pressure of the glacier butting up against the frozen lake created broken pressure ridges crumpling the surface. It reminded me of scenes from the Arctic, as I skinned across the ice parallel to shattering cliffs and ice pinnacles.

Rounding the headland, our campsite beach appeared in the distance, but out on the frozen lake visibility had improved enough for me to assess the state of the mountains around us. Although to the south of us their north faces were still laden with snow, to the north of us the south faces were in many cases bare of all but a few sparse snowfields.

It had been a strange day. Wind and snow had alternated with sunshine like cinema lighting, making a stage set of the scene. It was occasionally very wild, then incredibly hot, with distant rumbles that could have been thunder or blasting at the mine. Back at the tents Adele was feeling better, and she and Stuart brightened at the news that we had found a new and better way up the glacier.

Adele and I had been suffering from the cold at night and it was clear that the design of the tent was no help. I'd scrapped my previous expedition tent the year before but bought this one online, without inspection. Unfortunately, delivery was delayed and it had arrived by post just two days before we left the country. I unpacked it to find half the front door of the inner tent was simply a mesh panel with no option to seal it up with a zipped flap, as you can with the Wild Country Quasar. At night the warmth generated in the inner tent by our bodies was quickly lost through the draughty mesh. On going to higher altitude the situation could only get worse so I cut the hood section off my pertex sleeping bag liner and duct-taped it over the mesh. The inner tent itself was quite permeable enough. At last, we had a draught-free night.

Subsequent discussions with the manufacturer revealed that the designer had a somewhat simple-minded theory about condensation: that lots of ventilation would stop it. Quite right – but only because the air in the tent never gets to warm up enough for the water vapour in it to condense on the cold inner tent surface. In practical terms that's close to meaning that you might as well be curled up in your sleeping bag on the snow outside. Instead of condensing on the inner tent's surface (or the flysheet if it's warm enough inside the inner tent) the dew point retreats to somewhere inside your sleeping bag, dampens the down and you get cold. Back in the UK after the expedition, the tent manufacturer eventually agreed to modify the tent with a zip cover for the mesh panel, but only after I had used the term 'not fit for purpose'.

We broke camp in the morning, skinning across the lake and past the ice walls of the glacier's snout, to hulk our gear up the ice step at the edge of the boulder beach on the further shore. Easy skinning followed up the mostly dry, stone-scattered glacier with little left of the snow cover of yesterday. The line took us well north of the Dark Tower that dominated a confusion of crevasses nearer to the centre of the glacier, though inevitably we still found a few that needed to be negotiated.

Gordon discovered that he'd left his camera on the lake shore, and was on the point of leaving everything to rush back for it when I suggested he might find it useful to take his skins in order to get back up. Doh! Gethin manfully offered to tow Adele's pulk, which seemed to be the lightest, as well as his own, and Adele took over Gordon's so that we could push on to the cache while Gordon caught us up.

Branching off the main glacier

Glacier camp

More load-sorting was necessary at the cache before continuing around the spur to our left, but it was hot and tiring with full loads in the afternoon sun. Worryingly, despite a careful choice of route, the snow beneath our skis gave out some alarming whumps, and rafts of snow suddenly sank up to a foot lower, taking us with them. As the lightest of us and therefore the easiest to pull out of any crevasse, Adele was roped up in the lead. She set a good pace breaking trail until we reached a flattish area in a slight hollow below a rocky spur, which seemed to be a suitable place to camp.

Probing the glacier surface revealed a hidden crevasse so we shifted a little way to a safer position, marking the perimeter of the safely probed area with wands. Digging out snow blocks for walls around the tents didn't last long, though, as half a metre down the snow deteriorated into unconsolidated granular mush. Perhaps it was water-logged depth hoar crystals. We just had to settle for shallow placements and trust to the aerodynamic qualities of our dome tents to prevent them being blown away. From that campsite it looked from the map as if we could

At the ski depot on Peak of the 150th Anniversary of the Alpine Club

attempt peaks to the north of us, skinning glacier approaches and climbing mixed ridges.

Getting up when the sun hit the tents, we were away by 10 am, to skin up to the col on the spur to the north-west, all except for Gordon, whose headache was too painful to consider any exertion that day. The east-facing slope was crowned with an impressive cornice to the left, which had shed some of its burdening layers of snow in debris down the slope beneath. Snow conditions did not inspire confidence so we unroped at a half-buried serac and from that 'island of safety' solidly implanted in the surface we crossed the slope, one at a time, to gain the col on the right. As each of us climbed, the rest watched anxiously, ready to ski down in the wake of any avalanche that was triggered, to search and dig the victim out.

The col was defined on the right by the rocky south ridge falling from our target peak and a lovely ski run descended the slope from the col down to the glacier beyond. Not long but very enjoyable. With skins reattached, we climbed diagonally across the south-west face of the

Skiing off Peak 150th

mountain to reach another col at the base of the west ridge. Windswept, icier snow meant adding harscheisen to our skis, but it wasn't long before the ice was too hard for their teeth to bite and we found ourselves scratching and skittering about on ice like sheet metal. Finding safe stowage for a ski depot, there was no option but to continue on foot using crampons and ice axes.

For some reason I found myself troubled by stomach cramps, but pushed on slowly with Adele keeping me company, crossing a couple of crevasses in the ridge and very aware of the steep south-west face dropping away to our right. Stuart and Gethin pulled ahead, but they kindly waited just below the summit so that we all gained it together, then took the obligatory group photos. I remained on the summit to take GPS readings, establishing the height as 4836m, so missed Stuart stepping into a hidden crevasse slot and splitting his knee open as it hit the downhill edge of the ice. Adele closed the wound with steri-strips from the medical kit and applied a dressing. On reaching the ski depot, Stuart took off at speed, hoping to ski down before his leg stiffened irretrievably.

At the ski depot on Pik Ak Illbirs or Snow Leopard

The descent of the south-west face on excellent corn snow meant that all of us arrived at its base high on adrenalin, although in Gethin's case somewhat deflated by a perfect head-plant after hitting a patch of heavy snow just minutes earlier. Afternoon sun was bathing the slope ahead of us, descending from the col, and as Stuart started to climb, it whumped warningly. He then put in a safer ascent track, closer to rocks on the left. From the col, however, any hopes of a good ski down the slope back to camp were dispelled by encountering breakable crust, brittle in the falling temperatures on the shady side of the spur. Minimising the force and speed of turns meant most of the time we slid gently but anxiously over the frozen surface, but that didn't prevent one or other of us breaking through occasionally, leading to a clumsy double-take or outright tumble. Stuart arrived with his leg still more or less flexible, and Gordon was glad to have our company again.

We decided to name the peak in the Soviet tradition of long formal commemorative peak names: Peak 150th Anniversary of the British Alpine Club. After all, given the conditions we weren't sure whether we would get up anything else.

Next day Stuart decided to rest his injured knee, but Gordon was keen to have a go at the 4900m mountain to the north-east of camp, so it was a team of four that Gethin led out of camp. Skirting crevasses, we climbed to the base of a spur enclosing to the west a small cirque that formed the south-west face of the mountain.

Avoiding avalanche debris, we skinned up to a col on the spur, and discovered very fresh snow leopard tracks heading in the same direction. Studying the tracks, we could see that the animal had almost broken through the surface into a crevasse, icy blue under the broken snow, whereupon it had twisted on its back legs and leapt back and to the side. The paw prints, as big as my hand, then followed a line less directly to the col, the leopard somehow recognising faint traces of the hidden crevasse as it skirted its brink. At the col, the tracks turned towards a subsidiary peak at the end of the spur, presumably then descending into the glacier bay beyond. Despite scanning the surroundings hopefully, we could see no further sign of the big cat.

We continued skinning up the west ridge until it became too steep and icy. The possibility of continuing to gain height on the south-west face was prevented by crevasse barriers lying in that direction, so there was no choice but to leave the skis and continue on foot. I was tying my ski-related gear to my skis, cached in the snow, when I noticed Gethin was strapping his skis to his rucksack.

'Why are you taking your skis, Geth?'

'I want to ski the face from the summit.'

'Well, don't you think we should talk about that?'

'I know it's steep, but I think I can do it.'

'I dare say you could in the Alps with a helicopter evacuation just a phone call away, but this isn't the Alps. And to be honest I'd think twice about it even in the Alps with snow conditions like this.'

'It's a south-facing slope and taking a lot of sun,' Gordon added dubiously. 'It seems like there's a weak layer from what we've seen at the campsite and heard from the snow collapsing, and there's no reason to think this face doesn't share that weak layer.'

'But it's icier now under the snow on this ridge, which probably means the face is stable. Isn't it a matter of choice?' Gethin was very keen.

'You may be right about the snow, but we're not in a position to dig a snow pit to confirm that is the case on the face. And we won't be until we commit to it.' I was worried by his determination. 'Look, Geth. You might be able to ski it and you might not, but you've got to think about the consequences if you get avalanched and injured. The rest of the team will have to get you out and treat your injuries, and that's very likely to mean the expedition is over for them as well as you. It's just not worth it. On expeditions you've got to be so much more careful, because the back-up isn't there like it is in the Alps. I'm asking you not to do it.'

'Well, that doesn't leave me much choice, does it?'

I could tell he wasn't happy. 'No, it doesn't. But we all have to be team players in this situation. And there looks like interesting climbing coming up, so I'd like you to take the lead.'

This seemed to mollify him a little, and he roped up for the steep ice bosse above us, providing a belay for everyone who followed that was particularly useful for those of us with alloy crampons that didn't penetrate the bullet-hard ice as deeply as steel could.

Deep snow then forced us onto the rocks and firmer snow of the continuation ridge. It was good to swing up from handhold to handhold, kicking steps or balancing delicately on frozen-in rock flakes; a classic alpine scramble in the Whymper tradition. When the rocks gave out, Gethin led a couple more pitches of steep snow overlaying hard ice, traversing towards the summit with a big drop beneath. With an ice screw anchoring the rope at both ends, and one about halfway, Gordon and Adele in turn clipped Ropeman devices from their crevasse-rescue kit to the rope, to safeguard the climb up to Gethin. I followed at the rope's end, removing the ice screws on the way, my crampons tending to accumulate sticky surface snow despite the thinness of that snow layer. As the angle eased, we simply moved together, then coiled and carried the rope, soloing on across a slight saddle.

Above, the west ridge reared up in a final summit horn with steep ice to the south and a pronounced cornice overhanging the north face. Again, Gethin led a rope's length out to an ice screw belay, where it was possible to unrope and scramble on to reach the summit proper, keeping to the safe side of the cornice break-line. The GPS gave a height of 4887m; not quite the 4901m of the map, but it was very satisfying to gain such a hard-won summit. It had to be Snow Leopard Peak, or Pik Ak Illbirs in Kyrgyz.

Reversing the route of ascent, the team abseiled the ice pitches before I removed the ice screws and down-climbed, belayed from below. I benefited from the afternoon sun that had softened the ice enough to give better purchase for crampons. Back at the skis, we were soon setting off for a difficult descent on apparently randomly distributed heavy snow that would suddenly apply the brakes, breakable crust that set traps on turns, and isothermic snow that collapsed under the skis without warning. To compensate, there was a good long schuss down the glacier back to camp.

In the light of such variable snow conditions, I felt completely vindicated in my decision to rein Gethin in, but said nothing.

Ominous dark clouds quickly led to snow in the morning, and the obvious decision to take a rest day. There was some discussion of the future of the expedition in the light of snow conditions that were only likely to deteriorate as spring began to transition into summer. The pass to the east that we had intended to cross still appealed, and would allow us to evaluate the crossing better, as well as offering the chance of climbing a couple of peaks near it.

The weather improved enough in the afternoon for Stuart to test-drive his injured knee by climbing up to a knoll to the left of the col above camp with Gethin. Gordon was happy yo-yoing the slopes below the col to the right, leaving some nice wedels in lovely fresh snow, and it was pleasant for Adele and me to spend some time together without the pressure of an ascent that day.

Later in the afternoon Gethin arrived at our tent flap, wanting to chat. Stuart and Gordon were well into the habit of a nap before the evening meal, leaving Gethin bored by the lack of company as they snored. Less than half the age of his tent-mates, Geth would have plenty of time to develop a taste for the afternoon nap.

Next day we reached the glacier col in just under two hours, passing the remains of our snow leopard's tracks and some fresh fox tracks. The col had clearly been visited before; a few rusted cans bore witness to the probable passage of hunters over it in summer. The slope down to the lower glacier looked gentle enough for a viable ski descent, even with pulks.

The peak to the south of the pass presented us with a steep whaleback of hard ice, polished and gleaming in the sunshine. Gordon's

Climbing the summit pyramid of Pik Ak Illbirs

faith in his crampons had been somewhat undermined on Pik Ak Illbirs, so he decided to ski back to camp in our tracks. The rest of us took turns to run out rope-lengths, tie on to an ice screw, and offer the security of a hand-line or a belay for those following. The slope terminated at a narrow airy ridge, where Gethin belayed while I found a more technical route than I'd expected along the rocky flank to an even airier summit; a kind of fin on which we could barely all fit.

There was no sign of any cairn, so my surmise about the hunters was probably correct as this would have been an obvious objective for any climbing party. We duly left a small cairn of our own, constructed of stones scattered on the fin. The panoramic views included a hazy Khan Tengri and Pobeda, two of the 7000m 'Snow Leopard' peaks, away in the distance, and a partial view of the pass to the south. We had planned to return to the Petrov Glacier that way after crossing this one, but it looked as if it could simply be an icefall, so perhaps impossible for pulks. I was too absorbed in the climbing to check the altimeter, so just accepted the indicated 4720m on the map, and we later decided on to name the peak Pik Plavnik; Fin in Russian.

Reversing the route revealed that the ice had softened as the temperature had risen, encouraging the team members to pick their own lines of least resistance down the ice further to the right without recourse to the rope. I reversed the line of ascent in order to recover an ice screw and a couple of stashed ski poles, so missed the excitement when Adele took a 50m slide before successfully self-arresting with her ice axe. Stuart and Gethin had also suffered shorter slides, but unfortunately Adele managed to rip Gethin's ski trousers with her crampons in passing.

On the summit platform of Pik Plavnik or Fin

Back at the saddle we snacked and sorted our kit, effecting some running repairs with duct tape on Gethin's trousers. The ski back to camp was a fine long schuss with some gentle turns on corn snow that became heavy just above camp.

It was a warm night in which we listened to the glacier creaking and cracking beneath us like the movements in sleep of some immense cold beast. In the morning, I noticed a thin crack in the snow running under the tent and continuing for about 25m in both directions beyond. Probing around the crack did not reveal a crevasse, but it was an indication of how such features start when a glacier is on the move.

Adele led off at 9.20 am, skinning back up to the pass again, which we reached in light cloud and misty sunshine. The ice of Pik Plavnik gleamed wickedly as Stuart remarked, 'You know, if Adele hadn't succeeded in stopping herself, she could have gone right over the edge.'

'Good job I did, then!' Adele replied.

'Thanks for that, Stu. Now let's be getting on,' I added.

We headed north-west for a col between our target peak and Pik Ak Illbirs, being treated to spectacular views of Ak Illbirs' east face, studded with seracs, and north-east face, a sheer drop of rock and snow.

Outflanking the cornice by successfully crossing a bergschrund still on ski, we gained the col, left our skis, then climbed carefully up the steepening ridge. This looked broad, but fell away into a fierce cirque to the north with an insecure edge of soft snow over ice, whilst to the south the cornice break-line was metres from the edge, leaving us only a narrow corridor of safety between them.

On the summit, cracks ran in several directions, indicating fractures in the huge cornice that had accumulated over the short south face, so we stayed close to the safety of rocks that fringed the north side of the ridge. Cloud rolled in, but not before confirmation that the pass beneath us did indeed look passable. The GPS confirmed the height of the peak as 4815m, and we later decided to name it Solidarnost (Solidarity) as it was the only one that all of us had climbed together.

Our ascent track had become a 'sugar trench' in the increasing warmth as we wallowed our way back to our ski cache. From there we skied easily over the little cornice and down to the cloudy pass. A long schuss through scattered flakes of snow and spots of rain then took us back to camp by early afternoon.

The rest of the afternoon was spent debating our next steps. Whilst the pass was clear, the glacier beneath was a lot lower, which would be likely to mean higher temperatures and associated poorer, if not downright dangerous, snow conditions. There was no guarantee that we could cross over the further pass back onto the upper Petrov Glacier, so we might have to reverse the route, potentially a rather pointless exercise. There were no more peaks or passes to ascend from the present camp, so a consensus emerged to forget about the loop over the passes to the east and descend to the upper Petrov Glacier in order to explore that area, including the pass that we were uncertain about.

Next day we packed up and left camp by 11 am, finding very poor snow conditions almost immediately, and some tricky route-finding when skiing through crevassed areas. In some places our skis broke through the surface into crystallised snow saturated with water.

There was no choice but to camp on snow patches on the medial moraine of the Petrov Glacier. Water flowing down channels in the ice

Moraine Camp on the Petrov Glacier

was a bonus, and remained unfrozen overnight so that we could brew up more quickly in the mornings. Just as we got the tents up, strong winds came in, bearing snow. With little shelter and no snow-block walls, once again we would have to trust in the tents alone. Their flysheets rattled vigorously all night.

The wind had brought cold air to the range and at 6 am it was -8°C, so departure was delayed until clear blue skies encouraged us to head off for the peak to the south across the glacier. Our enthusiasm was soon dampened, however, by a series of loud whumps as huge plates of surface snow suddenly subsided – with us on them. Then a large serac-fall, tumbling ice and rocks down the flank of the mountain we were heading for, added to our misgivings. We gathered closer for a hurried conference, but not too close, bearing in mind the crevasse danger.

'I don't like it.' Stuart was blunt.

'Me neither. This is still early in the day after a cold night, and we're seeing the worst snow whumping so far,' Gordon added.

'And avalanche!' Adele reminded us.

'Yes; there's no doubt these are dangerous snow conditions' I said. 'We've been lucky so far with the collapsing snow, but the chance of one or more of us going into a crevasse is a real risk. So, what do you want to do? I mean, we're out now, and the weather is great. Should we just go back to camp?'

'I'm not keen on the mountain,' said Gethin. 'It steepens up towards the top, so avalanche is a possibility. But we could go up the glacier to have a look at that pass we wanted to use. Who knows whether we'll come back and try it next year? And we'd get a better view of the route on the mountain from higher up the glacier.' He was trying to inject some positivity.

'I'd be up for that,' I said. 'We're roped up, so should be able to cope with any crevasse fall. Avalanche is what's worrying me.'

'Aye, well, we'll get some fresh air and exercise in the sunshine.' Stuart was persuaded.

'Okay,' Gordon shrugged.

The attempt on the mountain was abandoned. As we gained height and could look back on it, a steepening band of rocks came into view across the snow slope we had planned to climb. Grey fans of rockfall dribbled across the snow beneath the rock band; a further deterrent to thoughts of an ascent.

A little further on we took a break at some rocks on the true right bank of the glacier. In full sun, we needed to drink, and inevitably snacked. It was very pleasant lazing on the warm rock, so when I suggested moving on, only Gethin started to sort himself out to do so.

'Tell you what,' Stuart suggested. 'You two go and have a look at the pass, and we'll just wait for you here.'

When Gethin and I arrived at skier's left side of the pass it was clear that an icefall lay to the right with broken ranks of ice cliffs and big crevasses between them. Partial views of this had cast doubt on our ability to use the pass to cross back from the glacier beyond. Now we could see that on the left, nearer to us, the snow slopes were steep but nothing like as broken, and would be no obstacle to our laden pulks. It was a pity that the bulk of the mountain had hidden those slopes from us at the higher pass. However, the glacier beyond the pass looked to be a lot lower than expected from the map, and down there snow conditions would be bound to be much worse.

'Can't see any obvious ski peaks,' Gethin commented.

'No, although there may be some higher up the glacier that we can't see from here. Very steep to the south, though. That pass in the distance I was thinking might be a possibility looks far too steep now.'

'Well, we're looking straight at it, and that always tends to make a slope look steeper. Not exactly appealing, though.' Gethin laughed, and I was glad he was there to confirm my impressions.

Concentrating on skiing back, Gethin and I almost missed the others in the vastness of the landscape until they shouted to attract our attention.

'Good job you hadn't decided on a nap,' I joked when we joined them.

Then the team skied back to where we needed to fix skins to climb back up to camp. The later stages of that ascent involved planking clumsily along a deepening trench of collapsing sugar snow, wet and tedious.

Another conference in the late afternoon sun concluded that there was little more we could safely do in the conditions. We calculated that another day in camp and a day to reach the lakeshore camp, plus a day to get back to Lake Petrov pumping station meant that transport could pick us up there to return to Tamga. Ayana at our agency, ITMC in Bishkek, should have time to make arrangements if I called her straight away on the satellite phone and set it all up. We were reducing our time in the field, but might be able to get earlier flights or would just spend some time in Bishkek.

Wind and snow suddenly swept back in, just in time for us to have to cook inside the tent on the hanging stove, yet later that evening it cleared to complete stillness and a gorgeous sunset.

Gethin had said he wanted to have a go at the big rocky peak to the east of camp, but the previous afternoon the rest of us had been negative or non-committal, so it was strange that although Stuart still didn't fancy it, four of us roped up on a truly glorious morning. Gethin was taking point and I was anchor-man, just making a quick check before we set off up the glacier, when I noticed something.

'Erm, have you forgotten something, Gordon?'

Gordon, checked his knots, felt for his ice axe, then hesitantly replied 'No ... I don't think so.'

'Er, skis might be useful.' They were still propped in the shadow of a head-high boulder.

'Oh shit! Yes, of course,' Gordon laughed. It was one of those moments we've all experienced, but it was all too easy to become absorbed in the spectacular surroundings.

We all skinned a short way up the glacier, keeping near to the moraine and thus avoiding any snow subsidence, then left our skis and launched onto the rocky slopes above. Adele and I took too long trying a *direttissima,* scrambling over balanced boulders, clumsy in our ski boots. Nothing much tumbled away beneath our feet, but it all felt like it might do so at any moment, so we retreated.

Gethin and Gordon were luckier. Taking an oblique line, they struck a shallow snow couloir that led them through the rocks to the summit snowfield. There, confronting a broad band of hard ice, Gordon felt his doubts about his crampons resurfacing, so he waited while Gethin gained the 4727m summit alone. He named the mountain Pik Mari, after the mother he had lost as a child. We were all back in camp by mid-afternoon, enjoying the spring sunshine.

Next day, we were packed up and away early enough to ski fairly easily down the Petrov Glacier, only to find our old friend the ice canyon had steepened and deepened with the warm weather. That meant it was no longer possible to skin up its side-slopes, so rucksack loads had to be carried and pulks hauled on foot. We then skied down the almost dry glacier, occasionally scratching over embedded stones and grit.

Nearing the lake, Stuart spotted that the ice had a melted to leave a margin of blue water. If we skied down to the point at which we had gained the glacier all those days ago, we might not be able to cross that water onto the ice, and would have to struggle back onto the glacier snout, then cross it, to reach the bay where we camped. The prospect was daunting, so instead we opted to make punishing double carries across a moraine ridge in order to be able to drop down to the camping beach.

Arriving there, we found the melted margin wasn't quite as wide as it had looked, and it was possible, with a bit of commitment, to jump from the shore onto ice firm enough to hold our weight. Although there was less of a snowpack this year, the season's temperatures must have been lower; low enough for the ice to be safer than in 2006.

Perhaps someone should have checked out the shoreline before we all committed to crossing the snout of the glacier, but you have to live with the consequences of your decisions, and hopefully learn from them.

Overnight, the margins of Lake Petrov froze solid to a depth of 5 cm, so we easily slid the pulks and skis onto the ice early next morning, skipping across to join them, and set up the towing rig; 40 minutes later we were unloading the pulks at the pumping station.

We all managed to get onto a waiting list for earlier flights, and spent three days in Bishkek before they came through, enjoying the comforts of civilisation. Concluding that we had made the best of the conditions, there was some satisfaction with our five first ascents, which had provided some challenging climbing; a fitting celebration of the Alpine Club's 150th anniversary.

Ak-Shirak's mountains would go on being spectacularly beautiful and it was clear that there was a lot more ski mountaineering left in the range.

11

AK-SHIRAK 2008 – AN UNEXPECTED RETURN

The following passage opens my journal for this expedition:

We should have been in Tibet but the Olympics got in the way. Or rather, a bunch of monks gone underground and pining for the meal ticket for life they'd had under the Dalai Lama's theocracy decided to mobilise and beat up Han Chinese, looting and burning their shops in Lhasa, sometimes with the shopkeepers still in them. Good publicity while the eyes of the world were on a mixed Chinese/Tibetan climbing team putting the Olympic torch on the summit of Everest. Not.

Excuse my jaded outlook. Having suffered at the hands of some of these robed thugs on Kawarani and seen the fear with which they ruled the local villagers, I don't share the rose-tinted spectacles of many westerners with regard to monastic rule in Tibet. I remember Pip Hopkinson telling me, 'It's no coincidence that Tibet was one of the poorest countries in the world while its economy was supporting thousands of monks doing nothing but meditating industriously all day.' Would any of us want a return to the Pope and his clerics ruling Europe?

To cut a long story short, after the rioting the Chinese Tibetan Mountaineering Association (CTMA) withdrew our permit to explore the Lhagu Glacier in the Kangri Garpo Range, and the borders of Tibet

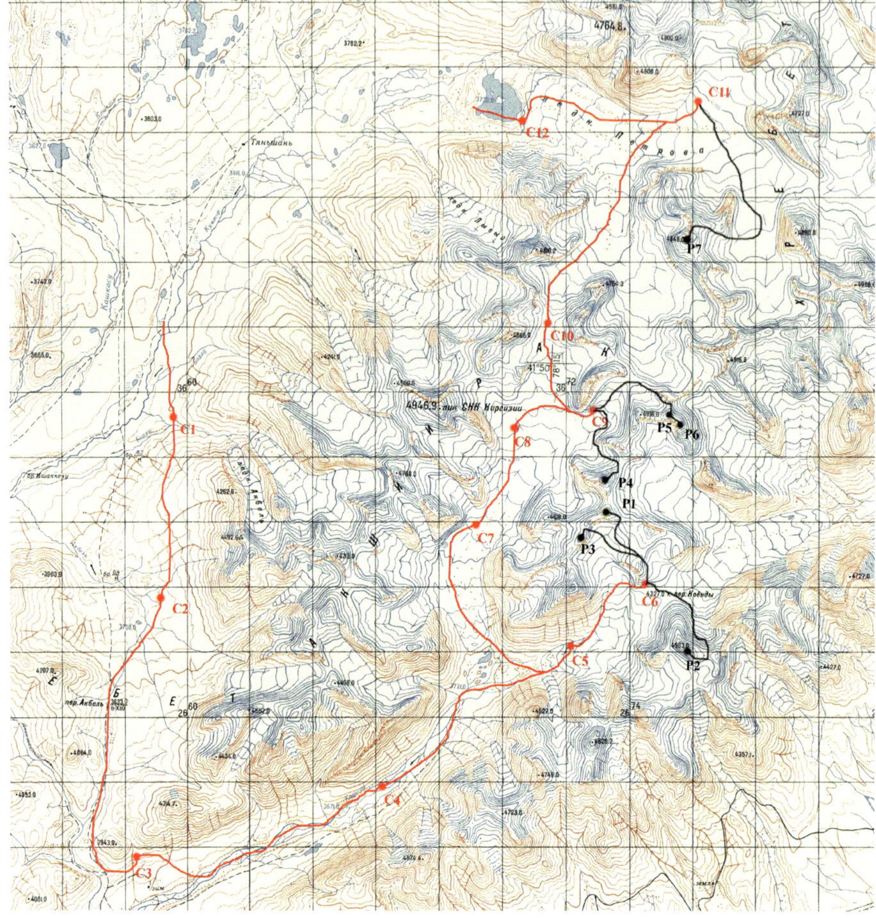

Ak-Shirak 2008 Route Map

were closed. That was probably a sensible decision; when I returned in 2009 to make another attempt on Yangmolong in an ethnic Tibetan region of Sichuan, our expedition suffered thefts and threats of serious violence from a gang of local motorcyclists who were only too willing to flash photos of the Dalai Lama brazenly from their cell phones. In 2008 our problem had been that the CTMA decision was made just three weeks before we were due to depart.

Three weeks is not long to organise an alternative objective for an expedition, but there was unfinished business in the Ak-Shirak range, with the possibility of a west–east traverse, and ITMC rose to the occasion. The Mount Everest Foundation accepted our alternative proposal and approved the change of objective for the grant. So there we were, Mike Sharp, Derek Buckle and I, back in Kyrgyzstan, together with Jerry Seager who had toured with me in Canada and Robert West, another Eagle, who had made committing ski traverses in the Himalaya and Karakorum.

Only it wasn't quite that simple. Access via Kumtor Gold Mine and Lake Petrov became problematic, requiring permission from the new nature reserve based to the north of the gold mine. That was arranged, then the reserve's officials tried to levy a $150 per head entry fee, which our agent dismissed as simply illegal – but the mine wouldn't approve our access without that permission. $750 was a lot of money, and I've always believed that such obvious exploitation should be resisted to avoid corruption and the undermining of local economies. Stalemate.

We held a team conference, and decided to go into the range from the south over the Ak Bel Pass as before, or possibly take a higher pass, scouted in 2003, to shorten the journey, thus avoiding the mine and its environs. If we 'happened' to go out that way, then we gambled that the mine authorities would be unlikely to bar our passage and we'd be gone before the Nature Reserve officials woke up to our presence in the area. Our west-to-east traverse would have to become an east-to-west traverse, approached from the south. Ayana at the agency thought it a good plan, objecting to any precedent being set which could result in illegal fees being levied for summer trekking in the area.

A trouble-free flight and transfer from Bishkek to Tamga was welcome and it was good to see Sergei and Julia again. Robert's veteran status was confirmed as Julia surveyed our equipment and commented; 'I see you are still using some old-fashioned skis.' Perhaps it was a reflection of a wider range of equipment becoming available in the country. She also recommended a visit to Karakol to ski the eastern mountains of the Terskey-Ala-Too range but that would have to wait for another occasion.

A 6WD vehicle that was booked to pick us up from Tamga made short work of the Barskoon Gorge and much of the way towards the Ak Bel Pass, bouncing through real off-road terrain before the driver jibbed at taking it over a suspect bridge. We had lunch huddled inside the bus, then set off in a cold wind bringing sharp snow showers interspersed with sunny periods. Two hours later we camped by a frozen stream that nonetheless had running water flowing through a channel in the ice. Camping on exposed grass, Mike and I were acutely aware of the difference in conditions compared to 2003 when the bridge where we halted had been almost completely buried in snow. Now, five years later, free-sliding tongues of snow had to be linked by wearisome pulk-hauling over thinly-grassed banks. This was all the more disturbing since Ayana had told us that Kyrgyzstan had had a hard winter.

On the flight out, I'd struck up a conversation with a Kyrgyz climate scientist returning from a conference. He informed me that while the world temperature increase was about 0.8 of a degree, in Kyrgyzstan the rate was double that. He was involved in research to try to establish why this was the case. Possible reasons included the drying up of the Aral Sea, salination of surrounding areas, and increased desertification to the south of the country. Crucially for mountaineers and the local economy, if the temperature increase in Kyrgyzstan reaches 2 degrees, then none of the glaciers in its mountains will survive.

Visiting Zermatt in 2011, I was to have the opportunity to talk to a Swiss guide who was also in charge of crisis management in the valley. He pointed out that if the glaciers disappeared at the current rate, many huge reservoirs would need to be built just to retain the equivalent water supplies for Switzerland that were currently supplied by glacial meltwater. After years of inaction by governments and disinformation from the oil companies, the world was finally waking up to the Climate Crisis; I just hope it hasn't been too late.

A cold night ushered in a totally clear morning. Mike complained of an altitude headache as we packed up, and we all took it easy, continuing along the frozen riverbed then up over alternating banks of snow and grass. The heavily laden pulks displayed an annoying tendency to roll on traverses, providing some interest for a curious fox that watched us complacently for a long time amongst the shrilling alarm calls of marmots. By 4 pm we were ready to set up camp, but stumbled upon a mining encampment with bulldozers busily reshaping the landscape. They seemed to be extending operations into this formerly undeveloped area. It was worrying to think that I had seen my first snow leopard tracks here in 2003.

Giving the miners a wide berth, we plugged on for another hour to the metal pyramid where Mike and I had camped five years before.

The elusive little lake that we had tracked down then for our water supply seemed to have completely disappeared. It had been a wearisome day.

Nursing an altitude headache overnight, I woke to the whispering of snowfall on the flysheet. None of us was very frisky as visibility decreased with the thickening snow. The way ahead was uncertain, so we talked over the pros and cons of route alternatives. Hauling heavy loads over a high steep pass would be punishing, but the lower Ak Bel option threatened to impose more grass-hauling, and the Kara Say River might well be in no better condition than in May 2006.

Later, as the snowfall eased, I stayed in camp to guard against marauding miners and foxes whilst the rest of the team carried caches up to the head of the pass. I passed the time reading and melting copious supplies of water for both tent teams. They'd surveyed the approaches to the higher pass and didn't like the look of them for heavily loaded pulks, so Ak Bel emerged as the favoured option.

Wind howled about the tent that night, scattering snow pellets against the nylon like gravel tossed against a window. Warm at first, later it became very cold as the wind died to nothing but as we packed up in the morning sunshine was breaking through the clouds. Yesterday's tracks had been all but obliterated by new snowfall, so the pulks slid more easily over snowy grass to reach the caches. On the way we were overtaken by a horseman leading a string of five horses, plunging through the drifts. He steered clear of us, passing without a wave. We took advantage of his tracks in places, but deviated to take the snow and favour skis and pulks where he had led his horses from bank to bank of lightly snow-covered grass and gravel.

Where the horses had gone over a gravelly windswept shoulder, we opted to descend the snowy gully that I was confident would become a frozen stream lower down. It did, but unfortunately, the stream then headed in a south-easterly direction, so we stopped where it was possible to link with another gully branching north-east to join the Kara Say more directly. There was, however, no snow visible on the intervening ground to make this link-up, so camping before the portage seemed the sensible thing to do.

The next day began with some heavy lifting; double carries of all our kit over about a kilometre of rough ground to reach the other tributary of ice, where we could set up sledges and skis for a rapid descent to the main river. A lammergeier floated past, craning its neck to observe us as we passed the derelict buildings where we had stopped for lunch back in 2006. Water bubbled up from under the ice where we joined the river, which explained the tracks of wolves and snow leopard printed into nearby patches of soft snow. It was also a chance for us to top up our water bottles.

We skinned on up the broad river of ice with none of the tedious portaging over gravel shoals that the team had struggled with in 2006, a benefit of our earlier timing for this trip. Another 9 km was covered before camping on the same gravel spit as we had in 2006, but a problem was emerging; Robert was having difficulty keeping up.

This had first been noticed before the descent from the pass, but we were all in the process of acclimatisation after the sudden one-day jump in altitude of over 2000m, as well as tuning ourselves in to pulk-hauling over less than ideal terrain. All of us had had our off days, but now on the open ice Robert was consistently falling behind. The evening brought snow out of nowhere on a keen wind as we cooked and ate in the shelter of our tent porches.

A sunny morning saw us pulking relentlessly upriver as Robert shrank to a dot in the distance behind. There was no doubt about the route and no danger of breaking through the thickness of ice, so he was safe enough but it was still worrying. When we stopped for elevenses at the confluence of the two big glaciers to let him catch up, I wasn't the only one who was concerned.

'Is there a problem we don't know about, Dave?' Mike asked.

'Not that I know of. According to his references he's done a long pulk-hauling trip in the Karakorum four years ago with no issues, and the referees were very positive about his fitness. He's supposed to be running regularly at home, toured in the Alps; you know, the usual stuff.'

'Strange,' Derek added, 'He's only four years older than me, isn't he? I did check, because I'm usually the oldest, often the only one in his sixties!' he laughed.

'Yes, but you do manage a lot of trips!' I reminded him, 'Plus you were a late starter, so not only are you suffering from less wear and tear but are very motivated to catch up on what you've missed!'

'We can manage with him falling behind here on the river,' Jerry pointed out, 'but we'll be onto glaciers soon and might have to rope up. We'll definitely have to keep more closely in touch, so it's going to be more of a problem if we can't sort it out.'

'I'll have a word with him and see what's going on, but we don't have many options. This is pretty remote, and an evacuation will take some organising. It might be easier to push on to the mine than try to go back the way we've come, although I'm reluctant to give up on all our plans.'

Robert arrived later, very apologetic and ate his lunch before we headed up the right-hand glacier into unknown territory. Frozen watercourses led through shoals behind a breached moraine dam, and we took another break where there was a good view of the glacier snout. It appeared to have retreated about half a kilometre in length and very much more in volume. The gentle tributary glacier falling from a high cirque on the right, indicated by our map, had become a hanging icefall above the main glacier descending from the Kyondy Pass. If that collapsed onto the main glacier it would trigger a massive avalanche.

We kept well to the left, climbing on to the glacier snout, and found a safe campsite in an ablation valley between the lateral moraine and the ice. There was water but it was cloudy with rock flour. Derek and I were both surprised that the altitude was still affecting us.

I managed to catch Robert for a private word: 'Is the altitude affecting you, Robert? Only you hadn't noticed that one of your skis had slipped into downhill mode as you were skinning up, until I mentioned it. And you're not finding it easy to keep up.'

'No, I'm not. And I'm not happy about it. Could be altitude, I suppose, but the pulk isn't running well. Poles might need to be adjusted to stop fouling my skis.'

'Okay. We'll have a look at it tomorrow. But when we get onto snow-covered glacier, we're going to have to keep much closer together because of the crevasses.'

'Yes. I know. I'm not going well, but these are my first long days out for a while, so I'm hoping to do better.'

'Okay. Fair enough. Tomorrow is another day.'

In fact, tomorrow brought snow so we took a rest day, talking through and acting, between heavy snow showers, on Robert's problems with his pulk, working on the poles and the traces attaching them to his pulk. Visibility remained poor, although there were times when the sun felt tantalisingly close, illuminating the shining clouds as temperatures rose perceptibly.

Jerry and Mike both set out separately to scout different ways onto the bulk of the glacier during a clear period in the afternoon, while I read a few chapters of Martin Chuzzlewit. The book came alive as Dickens mercilessly satirised the hypocrisy of nineteenth-century Americans boasting about the 'Land of the Free' whilst still practising slavery.

Snow and poor visibility continued into the following morning, but gradually cleared so that we could get away soon after 11 am, taking Jerry's route onto the glacier, which seemed to be the easier option. Jerry led the way up the glacier, crossing a huge crevasse with a thundering watercourse, or moulin, rushing down its length, but fortunately well bridged by snow at its highest point. We all roped up to cross the snow bridge one at a time; the idea of being swept down the moulin into water-worn tunnels under the ice was horrific!

Camp on Kyondy Pass

After lunch I took over trail-breaking, finding a way through the crevasses. Gaining height, I could see that the glacier was separating out into its tributaries with ablation valleys in the ice emerging between independent snouts. Climbing one of these tributaries to the north-east led to some moraine deposits and ice hollows west of the head of the pass, which offered a relatively sheltered campsite. Robert had kept up better, and all of us seemed more cheerful to be amongst the peaks in the sunshine. A strengthening wind with clouds scudding in its wake promised a change in the weather and the mountains to the south looked savagely beautiful with sharp summit crests and breaking icefalls.

The storm arrived, pinning us down for the next two days with occasional excursions in lulls in the weather to dig out tents and buried pulks. In the shelter of our tents we read, talked, sorted kit and gathered in the larger tent to share Mike's 'cowboy coffee' with real beans!

Finally, a sunny morning arrived and despite the bitter wind we could head up the glacier to the north. It was time to climb. A detour north-east to avoid crevasses led to a col, where we took a break. Jerry and Derek had been roped together as a lead team with the rest of us following exactly in their tracks, but from then on I led up the ridge, unroped, since there was no evidence of any crevasses.

Skiable ground finished at a sheltered bay just off the steepening ridge where we left the skis, and Derek led off on foot. The line of least resistance followed the ridge with some excursions onto snow slopes to the right and several short steep steps to be scaled, demanding good use of the axes. I caught up with Derek and took over the trail-breaking for the rest of the way to the summit. Waiting for the others to arrive and celebrate on the summit, we were able to see good views of Piks Kyrgizia and Koyon to the north-west beyond the Kara Say Glacier, which appeared to be even more chaotic than in 2006.

'Some awkward steps on that ridge, Derek.'

'Yes. Hard ice under the snow. Steps? Hmmn. Perhaps that's a name for the peak?'

'Step Peak. Yes. A clue as to what to expect!'

Then the others arrived and we all shook hands, despite numb fingers.

My feet and hands were suffering from the cold on the descent without any of the heat generated by the effort of climbing, but I still managed the camera to take some decent pictures. From the ski depot, we skied back down the line of ascent finding a mixture of ice, untrustworthy crust and chunky hardpack; needless to say, it wasn't very elegant, not least because it was our first pulk-free ski run of the trip. Back at camp, it took a while for my feet to thaw out.

The weather held into the next day as we crossed the Kyondy Pass and headed south for a route that we had spotted from Step Peak on the previous day. A steep traverse line around an ice buttress on the left took us out onto the glacier above an icefall, otherwise we would have had to climb by a chute to its right, threatened by serac-fall. It was still necessary to cross back above the head of the chute, but without spending much time in the danger zone whilst climbing up into the snow bowl below the west ridge of Point 4983m.

That ridge was also hung with precariously poised seracs, but at the far side of the bowl a serac-free slope rose steeply to a col. Derek, Jerry and I climbed it on ski but with ice axes instead of ski poles in our uphill hands, held ready to arrest a slip. Mike and Robert decided to stash their skis below and climb on foot.

At the col, Derek, Jerry and I had left our skis and were roping up for a steepish ice traverse above the seracs when Mike and Robert arrived.

'Hey, guys, where's your rucksacks?'

'Left them back at the skis,' Mike looked sheepish. 'I didn't think the summit was as far as it looks.'

'Yes; it's at least another hour away, and you can't leave all your survival kit down there in this cold in case anything happens. You too, Robert?'

'I'm afraid so.'

'Well, you can either go back for them, which will mean you'll be on the summit pretty late, or just ski back to camp. It's too cold to be hanging around waiting for any of us.'

'Fair enough.' Mike was still cheerful. 'That ice slope isn't the most attractive I've seen.'

Robert said nothing, but looked disappointed.

As Mike and Robert made their descent, the remaining three of us crossed the ice slope, avoiding the subsidiary peak on the ridge above, to reach a more level section with crevasses and ice ridges. Continuing carefully, we arrived beneath the summit dome. On the left bulked a

Approaching the summit of Pik Volk or Wolf, climbed by the ridge leading directly to the summit

huge old cornice on the south ridge overhanging the south-east face, whilst on the right an ice cliff merged into the north face. Between them somehow a steep snow slope had formed, narrowing to a kind of ridge where it bridged the bergschrund and leading directly to the summit. The slope whumped once alarmingly, but on detecting no further reaction to our presence we continued. Unconsolidated snow filling a bergschrund made it tricky to get over the lip and onto the summit itself, but after some 'treading water' and strenuous axe work, I was able to get my upper body over the edge, strike the ice axe pick into almost level ground, and swing my legs up. The others came up more easily with a rope above them, but the effort triggered a dizzying altitude reaction which had us all taking it very easy on the final gentle slope to the summit dome. We were at 4980m.

There in the clear air, Khan Tengri and Pobeda stood out, 7000m high and far away to the north-west, whilst serried ranks of mountains marched south to China. Several attractive peaks immediately north of us presented something of an access problem, because not far to the east of the Kyondy Pass the snow ran out into extensive screes and moraines that would mean we would have to carry our pulks over them. This was the unseen and unexplored section of the route by which we hoped to swing back west and continue the traverse.

The map suggested that a pass might possibly lead into the more north-easterly glacier basins by which we had hoped to reach the Petrov Glacier higher up on this occasion. Unfortunately, there was no guarantee of getting over that pass, and if we couldn't, we'd have to repeat all the carrying to reverse the route, losing a lot of mountaineering time. This was a worrying development, particularly as the effort of load-hauling and carrying had taken so much out of Robert. A day or two of double carries would do him no good, and I didn't like to think of how he might feel if we had to retrace our route from an impassable high col. The attempt to force a passage could just be wasted time.

Descending the mountain, we jumped the bergschrund and down-climbed to the ski depot, making better time in the consolidated snow of our boot tracks. Skiing steep ice down into the snow bowl was scratchy in places, and it was late enough in the day for the sun to have rendered the surface treacherous in the bowl. There were some spectacular falls before we learnt to recognise and link still-frozen patches of dense wind-packed snow and avoid the heavy stuff that suddenly applied the brakes to our skis. Following our ski tracks put us safely on the traverse line around the icefall, climbing awkwardly back and up a little to reach the head of the pass.

There was no sign of any seracs having collapsed but despite the sunshine temperatures had remained low all day, so that wasn't entirely surprising. Relieved, we coasted back to camp from the head of the pass to join Mike and Robert. Jerry had discovered more wolf tracks on the route over the pass, so we decided on Wolf Peak (Pik Volk in Russian) as the name for a mountain that had proved to be a challenging but satisfying ski peak.

Next day was warmer, with cloud hinting at a change in the weather, so we needed an objective less demanding than that of the previous day. To the north-west of our first route a peak in the middle of the big snow bay above camp had presented a triangular south face of steep rock to us, but the map suggested a ski approach to it from the north might be successful via a col and a snowy ridge.

We skinned up in our old tracks, then broke left onto a rising snow ramp leading, as anticipated, to a col to the north. Near the top of the ramp, I decided to descend slightly in order to avoid the possible collapse of a massive 'cream roll' cornice jutting from the col above. An oblique line was much safer, and easier on the lungs. The point where we gained the col was free of cornice build-up, but was barred by a well-established crevasse, almost a bergschrund, luckily sufficiently snow-filled to be crossable. We then climbed easily up to have lunch in the large wind scoop formed at the lowest point of the col.

Leaving the skis, I broke trail up the north ridge, keeping well away from any hidden cornice break-line to the east, to reach the summit at 4767m. There was a lovely view of Prospect Pass, so Prospect Peak was mooted as a name for this mountain as we lingered on rocks on the summit, enjoying the sunshine. It was interesting to rediscover the peaks and passes of my previous visit from a new perspective as they gradually blurred into the increasing haze, but not before we had established that the Kara Say Glacier looked even more like a crazy white dunescape than it had in 2006. I figured that keeping well to the Kyrgyzia side of the glacier should keep us out of trouble.

Reversing the route to the skis, we then enjoyed some delightful spring snow alternating with well-frozen crust, although conditions deteriorated lower down and we all fell victim to breakable crust or suddenly heavy snow at times.

Back at camp by 3 pm, and sunbathing with our shirts off, there was time to talk through a decision on our next move. It was clear that going over the pass could trap us in difficult terrain with no obvious easy exit or links available, so there was little choice but to return to the Kara Say and try to reach the Petrov Glacier via an unexplored branch at a higher point to the north-east.

'Not a lot to argue with there!' Mike remarked, over more 'cowboy coffee'. 'And we've still got time to do some packing for the move tomorrow morning.'

Despite an early start in the morning, we quickly ran into difficulties descending some nasty little gullies between ice ridges and moraine banks that had all the pulks rolling, but once out of those we skied

Skiing back to camp from Prospect Peak

more easily down the vestigial tracks of our ascent, gradually losing height. It was hard to judge the angle of the biggest ablation valley, and I came to grief coming off the glacier. Mistaking my speed, I hit a patch of heavy snow to crash with my pulk leaping through the traces and pinning my skis. Despite my bad example as a warning, others similarly crashed around me as I untangled myself. Robert had been skiing easily to that point, but was so unimpressed by our falls that he continued down the glacier to its snout, which was decidedly steeper than the line we had taken. He gave us all some worrying moments when we caught sight of him later, awkwardly clambering down with his pulk.

Once off the glacier, we free-heeled down the ice river, cruised through the gap in the moraine dam sind turned right to ascend the half-frozen watercourse leading to the Kara Say Glacier. As we were weaving between moraine islands, gravel flats and rubble ridges, the snow conditions deteriorated, so that the lead skiers sometimes sank knee-deep into a watery mush and had to fight to free their skis. There was a haziness in the air with a yellow-brown tinge to it, and Mike speculated that there might be sandstorms in the Taklaman Desert to the south.

Towing a loaded pulk, Robert was repeatedly falling behind again, but we all finally reached the snout of the Kara Say Glacier and thankfully camped on a level area just above it. I managed to catch Robert alone, and asked, 'You were slow again today; are you okay?'

'I'm all right in myself, but I know I was slow. It's the load-hauling.'

'Well, we've got more of it to come, and I don't think the pulk is the problem now. Is there anything specific bothering you?'

He sighed and said nothing, then, 'I think it might be the hernia operation. My GP said I ought to be all right on the trip but I can feel the strain in that area particularly with the pulk.'

'Oh. Right. I'm guessing your GP didn't really have a good idea of what was involved.' I paused. 'Are you running a temperature? Any signs of infection?'

'No, I've checked that the repair is holding; no swelling and no sign of any infection.'

'Have you got enough painkillers? I mean there's no other treatment possible in these conditions if there's no infection.'

'Yes, enough, and I know there's nothing else we can do.'

'Well, let me know if you run out. Try and rest as much as you can between hauling. Can you lighten your load, jettison anything?'

'I can't think of anything.'

'Well go through it with Mike and Derek; they're experts on lightening loads, and if you expect them to share the load at all, they'll expect you to have had a thorough clear-out of non-essentials beforehand.'

'Okay.'

I knew he was feeling down, but I had to make the point: 'You could have mentioned this earlier, like when you applied. We're in this situation now so we have to manage it, but don't keep anything else back. Please.'

And I left it at that.

Morning light revealed just how beautiful this campsite was, situated in the heart of the mountains, on the brink of emerging glacial lakes complete with miniature ice floes, and with the great frozen river stretching away towards China. But we had to turn our backs on that view to confront the rearing snow dunes of the glacier, threading our way through their scalloped ice cliffs and meltwater hollows. Each snow dome kept us in suspense as to whether we would find ourselves on a drop-off and have to retrace our steps or could wind our way down a slope or ridge to climb the next dome.

One impasse meant carrying skis and rucksacks on foot, trusting to our crampons, before going back to haul pulks up. Another steep slope turned icy near the top, defeating me and Derek, but whilst I had to anchor my pulk to an ice screw before going on with a rucksack load, his pulk mysteriously stayed in place as he followed. We then set up a pulley system with ice screws and rope to haul all the pulks up the slope and offer a hand-line to the others to ease the effort of climbing.

From then on it was easy enough to wind amongst less extreme snow domes and ice cliffs, although we passed close enough to the Kyrgyzia Icefall not to want to linger in the impact zone of any falling ice. All the while snow conditions and the weather deteriorated, and by the time we pulled into what had been the first 2006 climbing camp it was snowing. When I went to dig snow for meltwater, my shovel went through the surface into a kind of sump, and I then ran relays of pans full of water to both tents, acquiring wet feet and numb hands in the process.

I woke to the patter of occasional snow showers in the night, but the morning was clear as we packed up and set off up the glacier. The dunes were smaller now, but still presented some nasty drop-offs above little frozen lakelets. I knew that keeping to the west side of the glacier then swinging right to camp at the foot of the north-eastern branch was the safest line remembering the view of the glacier from the summit of Prospect Peak; but foreshortening of the view at glacier level created the impression that an easy line led directly east. There was some wrangling, and I could understand why; no one wanted to have to haul loads any further than they had to.

'Look, I know I haven't got a digital camera to show you, but I did check the structure of the glacier from the summit of Prospect Peak and it was very chaotic on the east side. I don't really want another day like yesterday.'

'But there looks like a good line running straight across. No sign of crevasses or many of these domes,' Mike argued.

'And if we can get through it would be worth it. Towing these pulks isn't much fun,' Derek added.

'Yes, but if we get caught in another maze of snow dunes it could take hours longer,' Jerry was wary.

'Anything to avoid any unnecessary pulk-hauling would be good by me,' Robert said, looking glum.

'It's a gamble,' I responded, 'and one that I'm so convinced you'll lose that I'm prepared to go on, on the left, on my own, although obviously I'd prefer company, as there may be crevasses.'

'Well, I'm going to have a look, perhaps give it a try if it looks okay,' Mike was convinced of the viability of his route.

The others watched him, undecided, while I sorted myself out to go on in the other direction. Within 200 metres, Mike came to a halt, then started to retrace his steps. Arriving, he said, 'Just there, where I stopped, it all looked very different. The only ways forward involved either a big detour or a lot of height loss. It's not as simple as I thought.'

'That's okay. Worth you checking. So, we stick to the original plan and stick together?'

The mood had swung the other way and there was general agreement, so I broke trail all the way to Point Anna, although I did notice Mike veer east occasionally just to confirm the state of the glacier in that direction. After a snack I struck off towards the foot of the peak dividing the glacier into two branches that we had unofficially named Peak Divide in 2006. It remained easy going despite a few crevasses.

Near the confluence of the ice streams, a confusing jumble of broken ice, moraine deposits and granite blocks shed from high on the mountain, barred our way onto the smooth easy glacier branch above. Some prospecting on my part discovered a bold traverse line down into an ice canyon from which a tough climb up rock-studded ice took us through the broken band, though the rope came into play again to assist with the pulks.

The peak that divided the two branches of the glacier was clearly granite, but as there was plenty of evidence of instability around a great stone chute we camped out of range up on the glacier itself. The boulders around us stretched in a ragged line back up the glacier to a higher point of origin from which they had fallen over the years. Wet kit was soon draped over the rocks, and once more there was water under the snow at the nearby glacier margin to make brews as we snoozed away the rest of the afternoon.

To the south-east of camp lay a glacier bay dominated by an impressive mountain, its north-west face hung with seracs, but a route seemed feasible gaining the north ridge where a rocky ridge fell from a neighbouring summit to a small col. Next morning we skinned up into the bay towards the headwall, intending to skin an oblique line all the way up the flank of the north ridge to the col.

At one point a direct line, climbing in crampons, tempted us with quicker access to the ridge but this was foiled by too much wallowing in deep snow and the discovery of a big hidden crevasse barring the way. A rapid retreat saw us back on ski and we almost reached the col before hard ice forced us to leave skis stashed amongst rocks and snow on a little spur just below.

Climbing on foot to the col, we then took a snack break before soloing, one behind the other, below the crest of the snow ridge. Descending a little to turn a rock rognon, where hard ice came to the surface we were forced to front-point crabwise to a small stance at the foot of the rock. Attempting to follow, Robert looked very uncomfortable. I couldn't be sure whether the lack of ice penetration by the blunter alloy crampons or lack of confidence with an ice axe was the problem. Possibly it was both. He stopped.

'I don't want to go on without a belay!' he shouted.

'And then what?' I shouted back. 'The next section is just as steep and icy by the look of it. Are you going to want to pitch that, too? And the rest of the ridge?'

'I'm sure I could do it with a rope!' I could hear the irritation in his voice.

'Look, Robert, placing ice screws, waiting for you to climb the pitch, leading on to set up another belay so that you can be belayed on the next pitch, all takes time in ascent and descent. And we don't have that time. We don't want to be skiing through crevassed glacier terrain late in the afternoon; that's asking for trouble. The odd hard pitch, perhaps, but we've all soloed what you're unhappy with climbing now. If you don't like it, turn back; wait for us back at the col. There's no shame in that; it's a good judgement call.'

'But I've been roped up before and been okay.'

'Maybe. With a guide. You're paying him to take you, and I don't know the exact circumstances – but here we're relying on a single ice screw for belays, perhaps more psychological than anything else. We're not moving together on easy ground, and it's not fair to put someone else in the team in danger because you aren't confident. Roped to one of us, we could have two casualties if you came off.'

'But …'

'Sorry Robert, it'll take too much time pitching it, and in any case it's too damned cold for hanging about on stances hacked out of the ice. If you're not up to soloing over that ground you'd better go back.'

Approaching Pik Volna or Wave

Climbing steep snow to reach the ice of the wave, with Kyrgyzia across the glacier to the right and the glacial dunescape below

I hadn't left him much choice, but I did watch him climb back to safe ground before I led off again, with the rest of the team following.

It was tough, but we soloed on until Mike found difficulty on a steeper section. His telemark boots were just not stiff enough so that his crampons were flexing too much for secure penetration of the ice. Derek gave him a belay for a short pitch while Jerry and I soloed onto safer ground.

When Derek and Mike came up, I gave Derek the lead again as we headed towards a two-headed rock outcrop that turned out to be guarded by a crevasse cracking right through the ridge. Fortunately, there was a snow bridge that held our weight as we crossed, but above, more steep hard ice proved too much for Mike. He was roped to Derek, but came a little way then unroped and climbed back down to safety.

'Too sketchy!' Mike yelled up, 'I'll wait for you here.'

Descending the ice of the wave

At the top of that slope, where rocks broke through the ice, the angle eased and we traversed to a small bay below the final ice crest rising like a great white wave above. Derek, Jerry and I climbed direct to a crack through the ridge, perhaps the remains of a crevasse, that was now a cleft in the ice wave that remained, cornice-like and suspiciously fragile. Derek was unwilling to go on.

He was, rightly, worried about the crest detaching under our weight and plunging us all into the depths, but I climbed into the ice crack, kicking through loose snow to the ice beneath until I reached the far edge where I could see what was supporting the ice wave above; it was encouragingly buttressed with stratified ice layers to a significant depth, so we climbed on, traversing rightwards along the crest and clambering over a small cornice to gain the triangular summit platform. About the size of a conference tabletop, it was quite airy, hung with cornices on every side at 4856m. Rapidly shaking hands and taking pictures, we were well aware of the time taken in this testing ascent.

As we reversed the route, Jerry remarked, 'I've never climbed ice this steep before!'

'It's certainly steep,' Derek confirmed. 'I'd normally be using two ice tools on a pitch like this, not just an axe!'

But they both rose to the occasion.

The ice had softened as temperatures had risen in the afternoon sun, so we roped up to avoid a slip, despite having the benefit of the steps kicked on the ascent. Mike had already started back and we roped him into the party as we caught up with him, continuing to move together with particular care as we rounded the base of the rock rognon.

Back at the skis, Robert's body language indicated some residual resentment, despite the fact that although Mike had been going better than him Mike had still had the good sense not to push on to the summit when his position had become marginal. Robert would never have made it.

Skiing down the steep snow-ice below the col was delightful until we began 'submarining' in soft, heavy snow reaching the floor of the glacier bay. That set the pattern for the rest of the descent; good spring snow broken by sumps of isothermic snow that seriously damaged our confidence as, by turns, we sank nearly waist-deep in the stuff.

Back at camp, we relaxed in the sunshine of a beautiful evening. The day had included some of the toughest mountaineering so far in the range, and Derek thought it deserved an alpine grade of D-. There was never any argument about the name though: Wave Peak, which would translate as Pik Volna.

On another fine morning, we skinned north to scout the descent from a possible pass into a new area and perhaps make an ascent of one of the peaks to the east of that pass. Skirting crevassed areas of the glacier, easy skinning led up to a big glacial col and onto a snow dome buttressed by rocks on the right. A steep slope lay below, but wasn't clearly visible owing to the angle and the overhanging cornice. The weather was so good that rather than make a more thorough investigation, the team decided to head into a glacier bay to the east surrounded by impressive peaks to see what was climbable; there would be time to check out the unseen slope on our return.

The peak above the headwall dominated the cirque, but it looked as though there might be a route on its north ridge. We skinned steeply up to a notch-like col at the base of a rock ridge falling from a subsidiary

Gaining the col on the ridge of Pik Cirque

peak to intersect with the north ridge that we intended to climb. There we left the skis, and I climbed out onto the west face, only to find myself scratching around precariously on hard ice beneath a thin layer of snow. Taking a line nearer to the ridge crest appeared to be safer, so I switched to the marginally softer ice closer to the rocks while the rest of the team either followed my line or scrambled up the rocks themselves. Skirting a minor top, I gained a broad, easier-angled ridge rising to the summit at 4966m. Derek was close behind, and we were both disappointed to find a small neat cairn.

'Not a first ascent, then!' Derek grumbled. Perhaps it had been the Dutch team in 2007.

The rest of the team was taking longer to deal with the tricky mixed ground on the lower ridge, and as Derek and I waited our eyes were drawn to the obviously higher summit to the east. A fine alpine ridge connected the two, and it didn't take long for us to give in to temptation and set off along it.

A short descent led to a snow arête that ran into a rock tower at the lowest point on the connecting ridge. The tower was turned via chimneys and ledges to the right with some pleasant scrambling although there was a little loose rock to negotiate. Beyond, a broader snow ridge broken by occasional rock outcrops rose steadily to the further summit snow dome at 5004m. There, we grabbed photos of each other and turned around almost immediately; time was running on.

On reversing the ridge, we found that keeping strictly to the tracks of our ascent didn't stop Derek from suddenly plunging up to his armpits into a hidden crevasse. He hauled himself out easily enough, but after that we roped up – just in time for me to sink my foot, thigh-deep, into another slot. Inelegantly stuck, I took some time thrashing around before I freed myself while Derek tended the rope. We just hadn't expected to find crevasses on this ridge.

Nearing the first summit, Derek waved to the others, who were sitting snacking while they waited for us, and we were soon all setting off back to the skis. Later discussions resulted in us unimaginatively naming the peaks Cirque Peak, 4966m, and Peak 5004m, though it was arguable that the lower was a foresummit of the latter.

Softening snow didn't help Robert's confidence on the descent of the mixed ridge, but he was fine skiing back to the pass. There, we realised that we still hadn't had a clear view of the slope leading down into the unexplored glacier system beyond, so Derek gave me a belay as I went to the edge of the cornice for a look.

As luck would have it, teetering on the brink, I was at the narrowest point of the cornice so could see the full extent of the slope. There was about a 100m drop of steep snow-ice. Even if we cut a passage through the cornice, which was substantial, getting the pulks down that slope would take a long time, and the peaks beyond didn't offer anything obvious in the way of ski routes. I was reeled in and reported back on what I'd seen. Some disappointed discussion explored alternatives, but in the end we resigned ourselves to going

Derek on the summit ridge of Peak 5004m

over Prospect Pass, as the team had done in 2006, to access the Petrov Glacier.

It was quite late in the day by then, and I was anxious about snow conditions; an anxiety that was justified when Mike went waist-deep into a slot on the ski down from the pass. He was tossed a rope's-end and pulled out easily enough, but we roped up for the crevassed area that followed, then skied down the rocky margin of the glacier to try to avoid any more crevasses. Still roped up, we regained our tracks of the morning and a little more confidence. That confidence was soon dispelled, however, when Jerry turned to stop and went in up to his knees right on our tracks, extricating himself but very glad of the rope.

Useful enough in those cases, the rope was in fact a mixed blessing, because it had also been slowing us down and threatening to pull us over, as turning was so difficult to synchronise. Both tendencies could result in one or other of us ending up in a crevasse, so I decided to lead the charge, unroped, down the concave slope directly to camp. I reasoned that there should be fewer crevasses, and that crossing them at right angles at speed meant the skis should bridge the gap as well as distribute each skier's weight better. That was the theory, but I have to confess to a strong feeling of fatalism as I set out, calling, 'Just stay in my tracks and you should be all right.'

Reaching the tracks of our ascent, I came gently to a halt to see how they had all got on, one by one. Mike was first, but had obviously not stayed exactly in my tracks.

'Why didn't you stick to following my tracks?' I queried. 'I thought that was the point of me finding a safe way through.'

'Simple. You went over a crevasse fine – but that opened it up, so I definitely didn't want to risk jumping the gap!' Mike was laughing.

'Oh right; that explains the sort of hissing sound I heard at one point. It must have been the snow caving in,' and I was laughing too. It wasn't that funny, but did defuse the tension; 'gallows humour', perhaps.

Everybody else skied down safely, and we continued with an icy schuss into camp, far too late at nearly 6 pm.

Packing up in the morning, we found the weather held, although reversing our route onto the Kara Say Glacier led immediately to difficulties. The steep boulder-studded slope was no less tough in descent than it had been in ascent. Then, climbing up through the band of domes and meltwater sumps, we found that the slopes we had slid down so easily were now steep little climbs, only to deliver us into another dip beyond. Finally gaining the clear glacier shelf above the sump band, we slogged on up to the head of the pass in close and cloudy weather to camp under the marvellously-marbled granite faces of the twin peaks rising to the east.

Overnight the weather closed in on cue with snow and high winds blowing thick masses of cloud, which meant that we lost the opportunity to climb those twin peaks. Instead, a day was spent reading, talking, and sharing 'cowboy coffee' in occasional surprisingly sunny intervals.

A return to fine weather the following morning saw us packing up and skiing off the pass down to the Petrov Glacier. Perhaps it was the shallower depth of snow this year that resulted in the pulks repeatedly rolling on the initial steep slopes, whereas in 2006 I'd been impressed with their stability.

As the angle eased, pulk behaviour improved and we regrouped to take stock. Just at that moment there was an almighty crack as a huge triangular serac broke away from the base of the ice cliffs to the east of us. I remember looking up and attempting some rapid calculations about the line of its fall, whether it would break up, and in which direction we ought to flee, bearing in mind a fall with a pulk could pin a skier down for some minutes. Luckily the serac had detached from the cliff at its base, where the retreat of the ice had left a kind of shelf. The serac's pyramidal form meant that a low centre of gravity prevented it tumbling over, and the build-up of snow as it slid forward formed a braking bow wave that, with its own inertia, slowed it to a halt after about 20 metres. We could breathe easily again, but it was definitely a moment to 'Get the flock out of here!' as Gethin, with his family background in shepherding, had put it in 2007.

We quickly skied down until Jerry came to a halt exactly on the tracks of those ahead, only to open up a crevasse right under his skis. He was unlucky in that his skis were parallel to and directly over the slot when he stopped, but lucky in that he only went in knee-deep and quickly rolled away upslope, swinging his skis back to the surface. There had been no sign of crevasses up to that point, but there were bound to be more ahead so we roped up, gently snowploughing down to the junction with the main glacier. Sliding sedately past the granite walls at the base of Peak 4837m, I couldn't help thinking that the range would be worth a visit in summer with the chance of new-routeing on rock and mixed alpine ascents on more technically demanding peaks.

Heading for the Dark Tower, our name for the moraine eminence in the centre of the glacier below, we could see that we could cross the rocks of the medial moraine easily at that point. Over lunch on rocks, warm to the touch, I could see Mike looking thoughtfully at the Dark Tower.

'You've got something on your mind. What is it?'

'It's that tower,' Mike replied. 'I was just wondering if it might be a pingo.'

'A pingo? What's that?' I thought he was joking.

'Inuit term. Basically, a pile of earthy stuff, in this case probably a dump of moraine debris, over a core of ice. The earth sort of insulates the ice from the heat of the sun, a bit like the way a capping of stone will shield the ice beneath to create an unmelted ice pillar that will create a lasting feature on a glacier.'

'Interesting. Good to have a polar expert on the team! Now you come to mention it, I remember an article about a 'fossil glacier' discovered in Italy that had been buried by the surface moraine that it carried plus subsequent erosion of the cirque in which it was found. The ice had been insulated on the same principle, and drilling out ice cores had revealed important information about the atmosphere of the planet at the time it was buried.'

With skins on, we climbed up the glacier, keeping to the right for further than I'd expected in order to find an easy crossing of the ice canyon that had blocked our way over to the campsite used in 2007. Once we were across the canyon, the shimmering mirage of moraine on the opposite side of the glacier drew us on through interminable collapsing snow that wore out one trail-breaker after another.

Arrival at the campsite was a welcome relief. The weather had held, although clouds had often cast deep shadows, dappling the snow and rocks of the glacier around us. By evening, though, the sky was gloriously clear with rich late light illuminating the surrounding peaks and lifting our spirits.

A quiet night and sun in the morning kept spirits high, but soon clouds were being driven in from the west on a keen wind. We headed south across the glacier towards the glacial ramp cutting across the north face of Peak 4837 from east to west, where more shelter could be expected.

At the base of the ramp, we roped up in a hollow amongst the medial moraine, then skinned up to the left in a wide arc to avoid the crevasses of a minor icefall. Trending back right above the icefall, we found our way barred by a rock band that divided the entire ramp horizontally in two, with a granite knoll standing out in the centre of it. Reaching the knoll, we saw that to the left the rock band was less steep, so, picking the likeliest line, we scrambled up, carrying skis.

Above the rocks, steep ice had us trending left to avoid it on an easier line, which again swung right above the obstacle. There was by then 100 per cent cloud cover, but the force of the wind kept the tops clear except for denser scuds that swept across the ridges as we pressed on up the ramp towards a col at its head. A subsidiary rock peak to

Moraine Camp, Petrov Glacier

the right of the col looked to have an arête of good weathered granite, offering a tempting scramble to its summit, but we were set on the higher snow summit to the left. Stashing skis in the shelter of rocks below the col, we climbed up and over it into the blast of the westerly, aiming for the base of the south-west ridge of mixed snow and rock.

Cloud had increased further, and snow showers were beginning to obscure the peaks around us. Robert turned back for the shelter of the ski depot to wait, while the rest of us climbed the snowy flank of the ridge, crossing a couple of crevasses to gain the crest. There Mike turned back, as the crest was hard ice broken by rocks rather than snow into which he could kick steps; once again, he lacked confidence in his crampons and made the sensible decision. Derek, Jerry and I continued on ice to the right of the crest, more steeply than I had expected, until we gained the top of the rocks and could follow easier névé to the summit, constantly buffeted by gusts of wind. Another neat cairn mocked our efforts, but it had been interesting climbing and we had no regrets.

We tried to take a few desperate photos, braced against the wind. I have one of Derek and Jerry grinning as they prop each other up.

We rapidly reversed the route back to the skis to rejoin Mike and Robert, before skiing back down the ramp. Breakable crust made the skiing tense, but the rock band loomed up quite quickly. Whilst I was scrambling down, my feet went from under me on the wet, gravel-strewn rocks, but my slide was stopped by my rucksack wedging against a stable boulder. Below, we skied more easily back to the foot of the ramp as the weather deteriorated further.

Crossing the glacier took a real effort in gusting winds and driving snow, with the cloud base down to the level of the tents. We reached those tents just in time for a lull in the storm to allow us to sort out kit and water supplies before the next squall hit. The storm continued all night and through the following day while I finished reading Martin Chuzzlewit; a good long read with the small print ideal for expeditions!

In one of the lulls, the question of the cairns came up.

'Who do you reckon will have built them?' Jerry was puzzled.

'Did ITMC mention any other teams going into the range?' Derek asked.

'No, they didn't,' I responded. 'And to be honest I'm not sure for certain who might have built them. Perhaps it was the Dutch pair who arrived at the same time as the Alpine Club team in 2007. They did say they built cairns on summits that they climbed, but never did anything about reporting what they'd done. I think they camped up on Prospect Pass then came back out this way, so Cirque Peak and this one would have been likely targets for them.'

'Not very helpful for other teams who might want to go into the range,' Mike commented.

'No. They were a strange pair. I emailed them to ask what they'd done, but never received a reply.'

That night gusts of wind still barrelled in to bend the tent poles and hurl hail like gravel against the flysheets, but suddenly there was silence and the temperature dropped like a stone, so that we packed up on a golden morning. As it was too cold for collapsing snow, we took the long easy schuss to the right of the Dark Tower, down to the shore of Lake Petrov at the far right-hand side of the ice cliffs at the glacier snout. The surface was sound ice, but there was plenty of evidence that the ice cliffs had been collapsing into the lake, and broken pressure ridges were rucking up plates of ice beyond them.

We skated over to the usual gravel beach campsite on the further shore where stones used to weight tent guys and pegs in 2007 still marked out the positions of those tents. It was strange, and welcome, to be back on dry land, however unstable, after so many days with the uncertainty of snow and ice beneath our feet and nights of solid cold under our backs. The afternoon was spent lazing in the sunshine and obtaining confirmation of our pick-up time next day on the satellite phone. The wind rose steadily towards evening, and by nightfall another storm was developing.

Packing up next morning in a tearing wind, Derek unwisely let go of his drying inner tent before removing the poles, and it bowled off across the gravel outwash like a giant beachball, heading for the glacier with him in hot pursuit. Fortunately, he successfully collared it as it swung into shelter around a shallow spur and slowed down. We crossed the lake ice to the roadhead in wild conditions, phoned through to security, and waited in the shelter offered by the pump station workers, brewing up in their portacabin. Kumtor security then took us to their admin centre, where the new head of security was again a Brit, this time an ex-policeman from Glencoe! They treated us to food and drink whilst logging our details as we waited for the agency's transport to arrive. As I'd thought, there was no problem about our lack of Nature Reserve permits.

Soon we were being driven to Tamga with interesting diversions to see an ancient carved stone and to make a visit to a local shepherd's yurt suggested by our translator who organised these logistics. It was quite touching to be welcomed into the family home with tea, yoghurt and jam, but our translator particularly asked us not to give them any money so as not to undermine the culture of hospitality. Reciprocating with presents of chocolate bars was fine, though. Hospitality can be a two-way thing: 'Thank you. That was nice, and would you like to try this, that I think is nice too?' But money would change the relationship into a transaction. One of the children took a shine to Mike, clambered onto his lap and sat there for the whole of our visit. The shepherd was responsible for all the flocks of sheep and goats for the entire village, living with his family up in these mountains for the summer season;

Derek and Robert on the Petrov Glacier with Pik Petrov in the background

this was a legacy of communal arrangements that may well have gone back to before the Soviet period.

Other legacies were harder to maintain. Further on, we passed a donkey carrying the sort of big plastic barrels some of us had used for other expeditions. Our informative organiser explained that the villages used to have piped running water but after independence there wasn't the revenue to keep up maintenance, so water had to be brought in those barrels from a spring.

In Tamga the garden was as lovely as usual, and Julia was delighted to see us, especially when we donated all our remaining bamboo wands. In Bishkek we also left our pulks for ITMC to use, as the excess baggage charges would, we expected, be more than they were worth. We asked Ayana to check the Kyrgyz Alpine Club records, but there was no information about those peaks on which we had found the cairns. She was happy to log our ascents and to propose our suggestions for names for approval by the KAC, although advised using Russian rather than Kyrgyz for translations. I've since read other reports of adventures in the area which indicate those names have been adopted.

***

On this final expedition, during 24 days alone in the mountains we had had our issues with weather, kit and health, but we had managed an extended exploration of new territory and climbed challenging peaks. Although yacht-based ski mountaineering has developed around the Antarctic Peninsula, benefiting from earlier work done by personnel on Antarctic Survey bases, I know of no other sustained exploration of a mountain range of this nature on skis. Our series of expeditions had nothing to do with making any kind of reputation, competing with others in making difficult, daring ascents that, once done, were unlikely to be repeated. Our expeditions had instead been operated in the tradition of Shipton, Tilman and Smythe, their members going into little-known mountains to see what they could find and how they related to it in small teams that learnt from each other as well as from the mountains.

The husband-and-wife team of Don and Phyl Munday made use of skis in their 1920s exploration of the Waddington Range, but did not do so in winter or rely on their skis as absolutely as we did. And there is something about skiing itself, both in ascent and descent, but perhaps especially so in descent, that generates a flow, uniting body and mind in an athletic, aesthetic experience, accentuated by the mountains that shape it. In the same way that many have followed in the footsteps of the Mundays in the Coast Range of British Columbia, I know from internet reports that others have followed in our ski tracks in the Ak-Shirak range.

The teams that went with me into Ak-Shirak were just going there to have fun exploring with like-minded people, and in the process have made a contribution to the mountaineering community both locally and internationally by providing the means for others to share that experience. It's a living legacy that I hope will not be abused in the ways that commercialisation has abused other mountain areas, notably Everest, or the ruthless human exploitation of resources worldwide that has abused the planet to the point where we may well render it uninhabitable for our species.

I have been left with an abiding concern for the mountains. In the space of just those five years I had seen significant effects of climate change on the area, and the words of the climate scientist I had spoken with on the last flight out remain with me: 'At this rate there will be no glaciers left in Kyrgyzstan in 50 years' time.' In the Alps I have seen the retreat of glaciers such as the Mer de Glace, the collapse of paths and routes as the permafrost weakens, and the increasing instability that threatens climbers – and even tourists on common popular footpaths – with rockfall. For these mountains, and indeed all mountains, there is the ongoing threat of irrevocable damage to the environment. All of us who enjoy the experience of mountaineering at whatever level have to advocate for the mountains' protection by combating climate change through our words and our actions. If we don't, there simply won't be any adventure skiing in future.

Meanwhile there remain opportunities to enjoy adventures on ski at whatever level each of us is comfortable with, but always aware that there are also opportunities for progression.

SELECTED FURTHER READING

Off-Piste Performance – Alison Thacker – Pesda Press

Ski-touring (2nd edition) – Bruce Goodlad – Pesda Press

Summits and Icefields 1 – Chic Scott and Mark Klassen – Rocky Mountain Books

Days to remember – Rob Collister – Baton Wicks

Climbs and Ski Runs – Frank Smythe – various editions

The Making of a Mountaineer – George Finch – Arrowsmith

GLOSSARY

While I anticipate that you will be familiar with skiing terms, I define below some mountaineering terms that may be new to you:

ACC	Alpine Club of Canada
bealach	(pron. '**bear**lukh') narrow mountain pass
bergschrund	crevasse between the moving ice of a glacier and the static ice stuck to rock on the headwall of a glaciated cirque
BMC	British Mountaineering Council
bosse	steep hump of solid ice
cirque	also *corrie* or *cwm;* the cup-shaped head of a valley formed by glaciation
col	lowest point of a ridge or saddle
couloir	steep and narrow gully
crampons	removable spikes attached to boot soles
direttissima	a climb straight up the fall line, the shortest route to the top
FRCC	Fell & Rock Climbing Club
harscheisen	('**har**shizen'); ski crampons
isothermic snow	snow with a uniform temperature of around 0°, meaning it remains unfrozen at depth. Once the frozen surface thaws, a ski will sink into a mush of snow, and in the worst conditions there may be wetsnow avalanches.
névé	consolidated snow; young, granular snow that has been partially melted, refrozen and compacted.
penitentes	('penny**ten**taze'); slender vertical blades of hardened snow, formed by sunlight
rognon	('**ron**yon'); an outstanding pillar or buttress of rock
sastrugi	('sas**troo**ghee') wind-formed snow ridges
serac	block or column of ice

MAPS & QR CODES

High altitude ski tour: Haute Route from Argentière to Zermatt • Long ... (outdooractive.com)

Wikiloc | Ruta CARROS DE FOC, COMPLETO

https://www.wikiloc.com/back-country-skiing-trails/
wapta-traverse-4178215#wp-4178219